MODULE 13

TECHNICAL COMMUNICATION

Learner's Guide

Agency for Instructional Technology

JOIN US ON THE INTERNET
WWW: http://www.thomson.com
EMAIL: findit@kiosk.thomson.com A service of I(T)P®

South-Western Educational Publishing
an International Thomson Publishing company I(T)P®

Cincinnati • Albany, NY • Belmont, CA • Bonn • Boston • Detroit • Johannesburg • London • Madrid
Melbourne • Mexico City • New York • Paris • Singapore • Tokyo • Toronto • Washington

ISBN: 0-538-68193-4

2 3 4 5 6 7 8 C1 05 04 03 02 01 00 99

Printed in the United States of America

I(T)P®
International Thomson Publishing

South-Western Educational Publishing
is an ITP Company. The ITP logo is a registered trademark used herein under License by South-Western Educational Publishing.

Communication 2000 Credits

Agency for Instructional Technology Staff

Dr. Alan Backler—Instructional Designer

Dr. David Gudaitis—Executive Producer

Lisa S. Williams—Editor

John Pesta—Senior Editor

David Strange—Print Designer/Compositor

Sharon Masters—Project Coordinator

Brad Bloom—Permissions

Amy Bond—Administrative Assistant

Connie Williamson—Administrative Assistant

South-Western Educational Publishing Staff

Penny Shank—Project Manager

Alan Biondi—Editor

Tricia Boies—Production Coordinator

Mark Linton—Marketing Manager

Dr. Carolyn Love—National English/Communication/Career Development Consultant

Peter McBride—Vice President of Publishing

South-Western Manufacturing Department

Project Staff

Margaret C. Albert, President, Matrix Communications Associates, Pittsburgh, PA—Senior Writer

Rhonda Rieseberg—Writer and Features Writer/Editor

Kenneth Goodall—Writer and Instructor's Guide Writer

Maureen Pesta—Literature Illustrations

Brenda Grannan—Cover Designs, Internal Graphics, and Literature Illustrations

Susan Booker, David Clark—Proposal Writers

Dave Coverly—Cartoons

Jim Shea—Project Evaluator/Developer of Student Assessment

Video and Audio Production

Bob Risher—Scriptwriter

David Gudaitis—Director

Brad Bloom—Assistant Producer

Terry Black—Videographer

Bill Crawford—Logo Design (print and video)

Amy Crowell—Editor

Lodestone Productions—Producers, Literature on Tape

Content Consultants for *Communication 2000*

Dr. Rebecca Burnett, Professor of English, Iowa State University

Dr. David Heine, Professor of English Education, St. Cloud University (Literature)

Dr. Patricia Heine, Professor of English Education, St. Cloud University (Literature)

Dr. Frank Kazemek, Professor of English Education, St. Cloud University (Literature)

Special Consultants to South-Western Educational Publishing

Anna Cook—Educational Consultant, Anna Cook Presentations, formerly English Instructor at Lerander High School (Austin, TX)

Helen Humbert—Business Education Department Chair, Kent-Meridian High School (Kent, WA)

Mary Kisner—Assistant Professor, Workforce Education Department, Penn State University (University Park, PA)

Theresa Spangler—English/Communication Instructor, Brunswick High School (Brunswick, GA)

(continued on page iv)

Reviewers

Kenneth Brown, Educational Consultant, (Lakeland, FL)

Jane Miller, English Teacher, McKenzie Career Center (Indianapolis, IN)

Michelle Walker, English Teacher, Roseburg High School (Roseburg, OR)

Sales Advisory Team

Trish Bobst, Pat Brzycki, Carolyn Love

The South-Western Educational Publishing staff salutes the dedicated professionals at the Agency for Instructional Technology for their tireless efforts and ongoing commitment to excellence in education.

Contents

Introduction

What do you need to succeed in the working world? The ability to work hard, solve problems, and do your part as a team member is a good start. But even with your best efforts, you will still need the one thing all employers look for as they hire the workforce for the 21st century: good communication skills. Your preparation for the working world of tomorrow begins today with *Communication 2000*, a multimedia course that will help you develop the reading, writing, listening, and speaking skills necessary to get and keep a job.

Module 13 of *Communication 2000* focuses on the skills in technical communication that you will need to solve many of the problems you may encounter on the job. Your ability to write clear instructions that explain complex processes and to create proposals that offer persuasive solutions to problems will lead to greater opportunities on and off the job. As you complete the activities, view the video, and practice the strategies of Module 13, you will

- take a tour of a Boeing plant with a technical writer.
- use technical communication to solve a problem with a Teleprompter.
- get a grip on instructions to relieve choking.
- help a child-care worker clean up the way hands are washed in her workplace.
- chunk your way to persuasive writing.
- go with the flowchart to plan a proposal.
- consider a poet's proposal to realize the American dream.
- propose a change in your chosen career.

LESSON 1

Technical Communication

A Video Lesson

Looking Ahead

What This Lesson Is About

In this lesson, you will learn how technical communication is used in the workplace. You also will assess your own technical-communication skills.

- ✔ Good technical communicators explain complex ideas and processes in a way that their readers can understand.
- ✔ Technical communication requires skills in speaking and listening, as well as in writing. It also requires a strong curiosity about how things work and a knowledge of the audience.
- ✔ Technical communication must be clear and persuasive in order to convince people to read a document, to help them understand it, and to enable them to follow the instructions or make suggested changes.

In the world's largest assembly buildings, the employees of Boeing rely on clear and concise directions as they assemble state-of-the-art aircraft.

audience—persons who will hear or read what you say or write; persons who will be affected by your decisions

persuasive—having the power to convince other people to do or believe something

technical communication—an oral, visual, and/or written process that informs an audience about the details of a topic

Viewing the Videodisc—Introduction

You are about to watch the first segment of a videodisc or videocassette about technical communication in the workplace. As you view the segment, ask yourself,

"Who does the writing in today's workplace?"

Introduction

Search 318, Play to 3511

Good technical writing makes it easier for a new employee to learn how to carry out a complex process.

Introduction: Discussion Question 1

Search Frame 3512

Introduction: Discussion Question 2

Search Frame 3513

Introduction: Discussion Question 3

Search Frame 3514

Post-Viewing Questions

After you have watched the video segment, answer the following questions:

1. Who does the writing in today's workplace?
2. What are four things to remember about technical communication?
3. How can you be a hero in the workplace?

Be prepared to share your answers with the class.

Getting Started

Cartoons, Chemistry, and Corrections

What do cartoons, chemistry, and corrections have in common? For one thing, they all start with the letter *c*, but they also share two far more important characteristics. First, they represent career fields that are expected to provide some of the hottest jobs in coming years. As the feature on this page shows, jobs as cartoon animators, math and science teachers, and corrections officers are three of the 20 fastest-growing fields of the future. Second, these jobs—and any of the other 17 high-growth fields—require a basic workplace skill: technical communication.

What does technical communication have to do with drawing cartoons, teaching science, or guarding prisoners? An animator may submit a proposal to a film studio for a new cartoon series, including estimates of the time, materials, and expenses that will be involved in developing it. A science teacher may develop a list of instructions for her class to complete an experiment. A corrections officer may write a memo or a proposal to his supervisor on the need for more educational materials for the prison population.

Whatever career you pursue in the 21st century, you can be pretty sure that you will do some writing on the job. You may have to write a memo or a letter, prepare a set of instructions, send an e-mail message, draft a report. . . . Technical writing takes many forms, and nearly all of today's workers are expected to possess effective communication skills.

Hot Jobs for the Future

To pinpoint jobs for the future, *U.S. News & World Report* interviewed dozens of experts in 20 fields across the country. Some of the careers they identified, such as computer engineering, are as much in demand as ever. Others may surprise you.

Field	Hot Job Track
Accounting	Business valuator
Arts/Entertainment	Animator
Banking/Finance	Financial planner
Communications	Crisis specialist
Education	Math/Science teacher
Engineering	Computer engineer
Environment	Pollution fighter
Health Care	Physician assistant
Human Resources	Training specialist
Internet/New Media	Internet executive
Law	Business expert
Management	Supply chain/Logistics
Medicine	Cosmetic dentist
Personal services	Professional organizer
Public services	Corrections officer
Sales	Electronics specialist
Social work	Grief therapist
Telecommunications	Wireless technician
Trades	Truck driver
Travel/Hospitality	Inbound tour guide

—David Brindley, Robin M. Bennefield, Norie Quintos Danyliw, Katia Hetter, and Margaret Loftus, "20 Hot Job Tracks," *U.S. News & World Report* (October 27, 1997)

Technical communication is designed to inform and/or to persuade. It is usually directed to a specific audience. The audience may be one person or a group of people who share

responsibility for a project, work in the same field, or have a similar need for certain information, such as how to install a VCR or assemble a jet plane. Some technical documents, such as feasibility studies and proposals, are aimed at individuals who have the authority to change policies or procedures or to commit funds to support a new project.

Effective technical communicators know how to write, speak, and listen well. They are naturally curious. They know their subject well—for example, how a piece of equipment works or how a procedure should be carried out. They also know their audience: they are familiar with the needs, interests, and priorities of their readers and listeners. Finally, they know how to communicate their knowledge in a way that holds the interest of their audience. Writing that is clear and interesting helps people understand information and concepts, even if the subject is quite complicated.

Based on what you have read, answer the following questions. Use a separate sheet of paper.

1. What are some common forms of technical communication?
2. What is technical communication intended to do?
3. What do technical communicators need to know?

Be prepared to share your answers with the class.

Proposals, Instructions, and Descriptions

In this module, you will learn how to plan, research, write, and design a workplace proposal. A proposal is a document that identifies some kind of need or problem and offers a solution. Proposals are used in many occupational fields. They may suggest changes in the way something is done; they may contain an offer to provide a product or service; or they may request funding or other resources to carry out a special project.

The very act of creating a proposal can be an effective technique for solving a problem. As the writer and other team members brainstorm solutions, they often come up with novel ways of addressing the problem they want to solve.

In the lessons ahead, you will also learn how to write summaries and process descriptions, both of which are common parts of proposals, and you will learn how to produce clear, easy-to-follow instructions and mechanism descriptions.

"The technical writing that goes into writing documents to work with this tool is taking very complex subjects and bringing them down to a fifth-grade level to where anyone on the shop floor can understand what the goal of our team is: to put the wings on the airplane the best that we know how."

—John Morgan, engineer, Boeing

Be prepared to discuss what you will learn about writing proposals.

Company Profile

Company Name
The Boeing Company

Location
Worldwide, with headquarters in Seattle, Washington

Mission Statement
To be the number-one aerospace company in the world and to be among the premier industrial concerns on the basis of quality, profitability, and growth.

Company Products and/or Services
Commercial airplanes, defense products, and space systems

Clients and Customers
Commercial airlines and governments throughout the world

Number of Employees
225,000

Trying It Out

Viewing the Videodisc—The Boeing Company

If you were looking for a technical writer, you probably would not start on the shop floor where jet planes are assembled, would you? As a matter of fact, you might not look there at all. But that would be a big mistake. In the next video segment, you will see technical writer Roy White spending a lot of time on the plant floor, where he talks with mechanics and asks questions to learn all about the equipment he must describe in instruction manuals.

"When the laser tool first arrived at Boeing, it came with two pages of vague, indecipherable instructions. It was Roy's job to teach himself how to use the laser and then write instructions so that others could do it."

Roy enjoys his work. He says it's like making "the coolest toys on earth." Other workers appreciate what Roy does because his manuals make their jobs easier and safer.

As you watch the video, ask yourself,

> "What communication skills are most important in the work that Roy does?"

The Boeing Company

Search 3517, Play to 14040

Post-Viewing Questions

After you have watched the video segment, answer the following questions:

Boeing Company: Discussion Question 1

Search Frame 14041

Boeing Company: Discussion Question 2

Search Frame 14042

Boeing Company: Discussion Question 3

Search Frame 14043

1. What communication skills are most important in the work that Roy does?
2. Why is it important for Roy to spend time talking with other employees on the shop floor?
3. In what way does Roy help the other employees do a better job?

Be prepared to share your answers with the class.

"Try to define as much as possible what it is that the customer wants. . . . Maybe he doesn't want a manual. Maybe he doesn't need a manual. Maybe he needs a tip sheet. Maybe he needs a video training program. But define the problem, define the situation, define the need."

Summing Up

Are You Ready?

You may not wind up writing instruction manuals for aircraft workers, but chances are you will need to use technical-communication skills in whatever job you have. Are you ready for that? You can find out by completing the **Technical Communication Self-Evaluation** form. Determine your score by following the directions at the bottom of the form.

You will not be asked to share your responses or your score with the class. Keep the completed form in your portfolio, and update it as you work through this module.

Technical Communication Self-Evaluation

Answer the following questions by circling the response that applies to you.

1. When someone does not understand a procedure, I create instructions that use words and diagrams (or drawings) to make sure the instructions are clear.

   4. Very often 3. Sometimes 2. Occasionally 1. Never

2. When I have a technical problem, I try to identify what caused it.

   4. Very often 3. Sometimes 2. Occasionally 1. Never

3. When I identify the cause of the problem, I try to find solutions.

   4. Very often 3. Sometimes 2. Occasionally 1. Never

4. When I find solutions, I think about how they can be put into place.

   4. Very often 3. Sometimes 2. Occasionally 1. Never

5. If the problem involves changing the way something is done, I try to identify the person who is most likely to have the authority to make the changes.

   4. Very often 3. Sometimes 2. Occasionally 1. Never

6. I think about this person's background and interests before I communicate with him or her about the problem.

   4. Very often 3. Sometimes 2. Occasionally 1. Never

7. When I write about the problem, I think about ways I can format the document to make it more attractive and easier to read.

   4. Very often 3. Sometimes 2. Occasionally 1. Never

8. I ask other people to review what I have written so that I can use their feedback to improve the final document.

   4. Very often 3. Sometimes 2. Occasionally 1. Never

Add up your score (Very often = 4; Sometimes = 3; Occasionally = 2; Never = 1).

Your Name ______________________ Your Score ____________

If your total is 29–32, you probably have great potential as a technical writer. All you need to do is fine-tune your skills. If your total is 24–28, your skills are good, but you have room for improvement. If you scored 23 or lower, you have work to do. Whatever your score, learning more about technical communication will pay off in the long run.

Circle the questions where your score was less than 4, and keep your paper in your portfolio for reference as you proceed through this module.

Keeping Track

On a separate sheet of paper, answer the following questions. Use what you have learned in this lesson to help you.

1. What is the primary role of technical communicators?
2. What skills should technical communicators have?
3. Why are persuasion and clarity important in technical communication?

Going Further

- Interview someone who works in an occupational area that interests you. Ask what kinds of documents he or she uses—memos, letters, e-mail, reports? Are the documents used to inform, to persuade, or to do both? Request specific examples of how this worker has used technical communication to solve a workplace problem. What kinds of documents were used? How were they developed? Summarize your findings in a one-page report. Be prepared to turn in the report to your teacher and to share it with the class.
- In a current issue of the *Occupational Outlook Quarterly* or the *Occupational Outlook Handbook*, look up the description of a job that appeals to you. From what you learn about the responsibilities of this job, make a list of situations that might require technical communication. Opposite each one, indicate whether the situation would call for a memo, a letter, an e-mail message, or a report. Also tell whether the purpose of the document may be to persuade, to inform, or to do both. Be prepared to share your list with the class. You may wish to keep it as a reminder that the technical-communication skills you are now learning will be highly useful in the future.
- Imagine that it's the middle of a long, hot summer, with no rain in sight. Weather forecasters are beginning to describe the situation as a drought. Just yesterday the mayor announced that all businesses and residents would have to cut their water usage by 20 percent. Think about the kinds of problems this will create. Consider how people and businesses use water, and list as many problems as you can. Then imagine you are in charge of helping the community reduce its water consumption. Choose one of the problems you have identified, and create a poster that illustrates one or more solutions to the problem. The poster should include written instructions for carrying out each solution, and these instructions should be enhanced with photos, drawings, or other images to make them easier to understand. Include a reminder to conserve water. Be prepared to share your poster with the class.

> ***"It's almost as if I have this giant erector set that's called an airplane factory and I get to go all over the place and play around with the things that help make airplanes. And I think that's fun."***
>
> —Roy White, technical writer, Boeing

LESSON 2

Planning

A Strategies Lesson with Video

Looking Ahead

What This Lesson Is About

In this lesson, you will learn how to plan, and you will see why planning is an important element in technical communication.

- The planning process involves four steps: identifying the problem, devising a solution, dividing the solution into tasks, and creating a schedule for completing the tasks.
- The "5 Ws and an H" technique and brainstorming are helpful strategies for identifying problems and their solutions.
- In written workplace communication, planning includes a fifth step: finding the appropriate form for the document that will be created—e-mail, letter, memo, report, or proposal.

Key Ideas

brainstorming—the unrestrained offering of ideas by members of a group seeking to solve a problem

feasibility report—a document that defines a problem, offers criteria for solving it, suggests possible solutions, and then recommends the best solution

memo (or memorandum)—an informal written message, usually sent within an organization

retailer—a person or business that sells goods or articles directly to consumers

spontaneous—without thought or planning

Playing It by Ear

Have you ever brushed off the idea of planning by saying, "Oh, let's just play it by ear"? Sometimes it's fine to be spontaneous—to do something on the spur of the moment without thinking about it or planning for it. But you're usually better off if you look ahead—figure out where you want to go and decide on the best way to get there. If you have a long research paper due next month for one of your classes, you'll probably do a better job and experience a lot less stress by planning ahead instead of waiting till the last minute.

Think of a time when you didn't plan ahead and, as a result, ran into problems that you could have avoided if you had done some planning. In your journal, describe the incident. Then describe the planning that you should have done in advance.

Be prepared to share your experience with the class.

Getting Started

A Primer on Planning

In the workplace, planning is a way of solving problems. It is also a way of averting problems by anticipating what might go wrong and heading off trouble before it develops. Planning is a regular and often ongoing activity in most occupational areas. Clothing retailers, for example, must decide in October what spring fashions they will display in February, and the designers who produce the spring lines must come up with their plans even earlier. Farmers must decide in winter what crops they will plant in the spring (see "A Farmer's Calendar," page 12). Companies and organizations of all types frequently engage in what they call long-range planning, in which they consider their own strengths and weaknesses and assess the threats and opportunities that exist in the marketplace.

Whether planning occurs on a midwestern farm, in the executive suite of a Manhattan corporation, or in your own personal life, the process is the same. It consists of four major steps:

Identify the problem or goal. When you start out on a trip, you need to know what your destination is. Otherwise, how will you know what route to take or how long the trip will be? The same holds true for planning of any kind. The first step is to identify your goal or the problem that you intend to solve. That's not as easy as it sounds.

A good way to be sure that you're headed in the right direction is to use the "5 Ws and an H" questioning technique. Based on a verse by poet Rudyard Kipling, this formula is often used by journalists to make sure that all the key details are included in a news story: who, what, when, where, why, and how. Here's how it works in planning:

- Ask *who?* Who is involved in the problem? Who are the stakeholders? Who is responsible for the problem?

Document Planning

When you plan, you need to make decisions about a variety of elements: content, purpose, task, audience, constraints, organization, and design. Initially you'll probably define your subject and determine your document's scope. You'll probably also examine the document's objective and carefully analyze the intended audience. After identifying the purpose and audience, you'll identify the task. As your work on a document progresses, you can change your plans, but you must begin with a sense of what you're doing and where you're going, in part because changes in one element influence the other elements.

—Adapted from Rebecca E. Burnett, *Technical Communication*, 3d ed. (Belmont, CA: Wadsworth, 1994)

- Ask *what?* What do we need to know about the problem? What is the nature of the problem?
- Ask *when?* When does the problem occur?
- Ask *where?* Where does the problem occur?
- Ask *why?* Why are things happening the way they are? (Be careful not to point a finger at a person by asking, "Why did you do this?")
- Ask *how?* How does the problem happen?

Once you have answered the 5 Ws and an H, you should be able to identify the problem and what is causing it.

Identify the solution. Most problems don't have easy solutions; if they did, they wouldn't be problems for long. A variety of viewpoints is usually helpful in finding a solution, and one good way to collect ideas is through brainstorming. Brainstorming is a process by which all the people involved sit down together and share their ideas. Everyone is encouraged to offer whatever ideas come to mind—no matter how far-fetched they may seem—and each person builds on what others have said. Most groups eventually come up with a workable solution to even the most difficult problems if they engage in brainstorming.

Divide the solution into tasks and gather the necessary information. To put the solution into effect, it must be broken down into specific tasks, and these tasks must be assigned to appropriate individuals who can carry them out. To know what the tasks are involves gathering, organizing, and recording relevant information.

Create a schedule for completing the tasks. One way to do this is to develop a time line. Start with the deadline for completion, and then work your way back, assigning the time needed to accomplish each task until you have reached the first task. How many days, weeks, or months will all of the tasks take to complete? Subtract that amount from the deadline, and you will have the date when the tasks should begin. Some problems occur at regular intervals and have definite deadlines.

Planning for technical communication involves each of the four steps, but it also includes a fifth step: deciding what kinds of written documents are needed to complete the tasks and solve the problems.

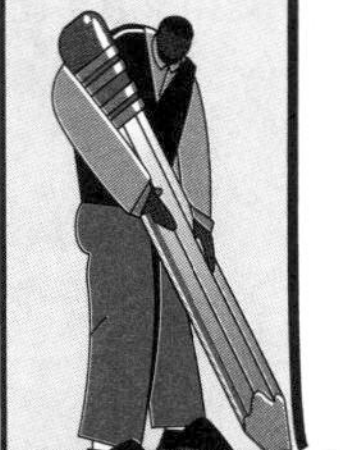

Strategies for Planning for an Uncertain Future

Some problems occur not because a company fails to plan but because it fails to plan for an uncertain future. Some planning experts believe problems can occur when a company bases its plan for the future on past experience. How do you avoid these pitfalls of experience?

- If you suspect your environment is changing, get help fast from someone who is familiar with the change.
- Think up ways that a competitor might put you out of business. In other words, think of new products or services *before* your competitor does.
- Read stuff that's totally unrelated to your industry. Hallmark designers created the irreverent "Shoe Box" line of cards using topics culled from the *National Enquirer*—not Hallmark's usual source of inspiration.
- Instead of listening to what customers say they want, study their habits and everyday experiences, their frustrations, and failures.

—Adapted from James Champy, "Mark Twain, Business Consultant," *Forbes* (August 11, 1997)

A Farmer's Calendar

Cash-grain farmer Darrell Schaper cuts a diverted acre of green oats. Part of the planning process in farming may involve planning *not* to farm a number of acres in an effort to keep crop prices stable. These diverted acres will be planted with a ground-cover crop to prevent erosion, but the crop will be cut down before it ripens.

August

Plan on whether or not to lease land again. Leases expire September 1.

Buy propane for crop dryer because it is cheaper with special discounts. It will be used in October.

October

Test soil and analyze fertilizer requirements.

Harvest crop and put on fall fertilizer. Harvest soybeans as soon as they are dry. Windstorms or snow can knock a crop down, but they're not as critical a hazard to corn. Harvest corn when it is down to 24 percent moisture content.

Fall tillage is based on crop in field. Plow cornstalk residue in fall. Till in spring if bean stubble.

Plan what crop will be planted in each field next year.

Winter

Plan year-end tax strategy in November and December.

See what seed dealers' field tests show in local plot. Plan what varieties of seed corn to buy. Buy in December for tax purposes. Could also buy in January/February when dealers offer special prices.

Size up machinery. May send in equipment to be repaired to avoid breakdowns in the field. May buy new equipment.

Check bins for grain quality. Aerate if necessary.

Plan operating budget for next year with creditor.

March

Federal multiperil crop insurance must be bought by March 15. Hail insurance can be taken out at any time but is not effective for 24 hours after purchase.

Make decisions on herbicides—what kind, when to use, and how to use. Decide what worked last year, and see what new products are out.

Service tractors, drills, planters, and other equipment.

April–May

Apply nitrogen fertilizer and soil-applied herbicides.

Plant corn when walnut leaves are the size of squirrel ears or when the soil at four inches deep is 50°F.

June

Cultivate the crop before it gets too big, ground is crusted, or weeds take over.

Observe weedy areas and spray.

Certify planted acres with USDA Farm Service Agency.

Summer

Get combine overhauled. Clean bins for new crop no later than September. Watch crop to see how it is maturing.

Scout fields for insect infestation, herbicide failure, and stress from weather conditions.

Other Considerations

Marketing is a year-round consideration. A farmer needs to follow market trends and devise a plan to sell crops in an orderly and profitable manner. This usually means selling at intervals, several times a year.

Income-tax management is a constant consideration that can cause major changes in the business.

An operating budget with cash-flow projections is mandatory. A farmer needs a line of credit.

—Darrell Schaper, cash-grain farmer and farm consultant/accountant, Brit, Iowa

Written documents in the workplace include e-mail, letters, memos, feasibility reports, and proposals. Each type of document has its own specific purpose, and knowing which one to use at any point in the planning process is key to the effectiveness of the planning. The following chart provides general guidelines for choosing among the various written documents.

If you need to . . .	and your audience is . . .	consider using . . .
determine how others have handled the problem	colleagues, co-workers in a regional office	e-mail or a letter
determine the nature of the problem	a client	a letter
identify what tasks need to be done and who will do them	co-workers involved in solving the problem	a memo or e-mail
define a problem, offer criteria for solving it, suggest possible solutions, and recommend the best solution	a supervisor, a client	a feasibility report
seek support for the best solution	a supervisor, a client	a proposal

"This isn't the first time we've had technical problems that new employees couldn't handle. I don't blame you, Carmen."
—**Jack Teller, technical director, Channel 3**

Using what you have read, answer the following questions:

1 What is a good technique for identifying a problem?

2 What is a good technique for generating solutions to a problem?

3 How do the circumstances differ for using a feasibility study and a proposal?

Be prepared to share your answers with the class.

Trying It Out

Viewing the Videodisc—On the Air with Channel 3

You are about to watch a video that takes you to a TV studio where you watch as the crew puts on the evening news. All goes well at first—but watch out! Before the show is over, everyone will be in deep trouble.

Your job will be to determine just what the problem is. To do this, you will use the "5 Ws and an H" technique you learned about in **Getting Started**. As you watch the video, ask yourself these questions about the problem: who, what, when, where, why, and how?

On the Air with Channel 3

Search 14046, Play to 20690

Post-Viewing Activity

Complete the **Defining a Problem with 5 Ws and an H** form. Then identify the basic cause of the problem that rattled the staff at Channel 3.

Be prepared to share your answers with the class and to reach a consensus on what caused the problem.

Brainstorming

In other lessons of this module, you will have an opportunity to address the Teleprompter problem. You will learn to gather the information you need and to write instructions, mechanism and process descriptions, and a proposal. All of these skills will help you solve the problem.

But first, try your wits at brainstorming. Consider possible solutions to the Teleprompter problem. See how many possible solutions you and other students can come up with.

Leave the list of possible solutions posted while you watch the second segment of the videodisc. You will be asked to compare the results of your brainstorming session with those of the TV news staff.

A behind-the-scenes problem with the evening newscast leaves Channel 3 sportscaster Stu Kapowski fumbling for the scores.

Defining a Problem with 5 Ws and an H

The Questions		Your Answers
Who . . .	is involved in the problem? Who are the stakeholders? Who is responsible for the problem?	
What . . .	do we need to know about the problem? What is the nature of the problem?	
When . . .	does the problem occur?	
Where . . .	does the problem occur?	
Why . . .	are things happening the way they are? (Be careful not to point a finger at a person by asking, "Why did you do this?")	
How . . .	does the problem happen?	

Identify the underlying cause of the problem: ______________________________

Planning a Solution

Search 20693, Play to 26513

"We evaluated several ideas based on cost, time, and effectiveness—the three key factors the operations manager will look for."

Summing Up

Viewing the Videodisc—Planning a Solution

This video segment shows how the Channel 3 news staff identified the problem with the Teleprompter, brainstormed possible solutions, and came up with a plan to avoid similar catastrophes in the future. As you watch this segment, ask yourself,

"What did the news staff decide to do to solve the problem?"

Planning a Solution:
Discussion Question 1

Search Frame 26514

Planning a Solution:
Discussion Question 2

Search Frame 26515

Planning a Solution:
Discussion Question 3

Search Frame 26516

Post-Viewing Questions

After you've watched the video segment, answer the following questions:

1. How did the news staff's definition of the problem compare with yours?
2. Why did the people in the video choose to write a proposal to solve the problem?
3. How did they determine the audience for their proposal?

Scenario Planning

When I look back on my own errors, it's that the boundaries of the problem were drawn too narrowly. The second mistake most of us make is imagining that the future is predictable. What we can do is develop what we call scenarios—short stories about what tomorrow may look like. But they are also powerful planning tools that help us think systematically about the different possibilities and how we might best respond.

—Adapted from an interview with Global Business Network cofounders Peter Schwartz (quoted) and Stewart Brand by Robert McGarvey, "Tomorrow Land," *Entrepreneur* (February 1996)

4 The employees directed their plan to the operations manager. How did the choice of this audience influence their recommendations and the way they were presented?

Be prepared to share your critique with the class.

> ***"Each problem has hidden in it an opportunity so powerful that it literally dwarfs the problem. The greatest success stories were created by people who recognized a problem and turned it into an opportunity."***
>
> —Joseph Sugarman, American business executive

Keeping Track

On a separate sheet of paper, answer the following questions. Use what you have learned in this lesson to help you.

1 What are the four steps in the planning process?

2 What is the "5 Ws and an H" strategy, and how does it assist in planning?

3 What is the fifth step when the planning is in technical communication?

Going Further

- Think of a problem or a goal in your own life. It could be a school paper that is due in two weeks, the need to save enough money over the next six months to make a tuition payment, or the responsibility for planning a party or a trip. Using what you have learned in this lesson about planning, develop a plan for accomplishing your goal. Break it down into separate tasks, and schedule those tasks over a reasonable time period. Then, using the computer, create a work plan (or "to do" list) that will tell you what to do each day in order to reach your long-term goal. If other people are involved, be sure that responsibility is assigned to each task. As you create your plan, think of ways to make it more usable and more attractive—for example, you may want to design it in the form of a calendar or provide checkoff boxes beside each item.

- Planning also involves anticipating the unexpected. What do mail-order businesses do if the delivery company they use goes on strike? What do farmers do if an early frost threatens their crops? What would you do if it rained on the only day you and your friends could go to the fair? Planning for the unexpected involves answering two questions: "What could go wrong?" and "How could I respond to the problem?" Practice planning for the unexpected by choosing a job in a vocational area that interests you. On a sheet of paper, make three columns. Label the first one "Tasks," the second one "What could go wrong?" and the third "How could I respond?" Then determine what your tasks would be if you had the job. Look for this information in your library or on the Internet, or interview someone who works in that area. List the tasks in the first column. Then complete the second column by listing any problems that may interfere with your completing each task. Think about possible solutions to these problems, and list them in the third column. Be creative when thinking about possible problems and solutions. Remember: An umbrella isn't the only thing that can keep you dry in a downpour. Be prepared to share your strategies for handling the unexpected with the class.

- Look for more information on planning in your library, on the Internet, and from other people. Because planning is such a basic part of solving problems, you'll have quite a selection of materials from which to choose. Read through the material you gather, and identify strategies and tips you could use to complete one or more of the planning stages. Then create a planning tip sheet that lists the five strategies and tips you are most likely to use. Provide a brief description of how the tip would help you complete one or more of the planning stages. Be prepared to share your planning tip sheet with the class.

Plan Talk

"If you don't know where you are going, you will probably end up somewhere else."

—Laurence J. Peter,
Canadian psychologist

"Even the best team, without a sound plan, can't score."

—Woody Hayes,
American football coach

"What is the use of running when we are not on the right road?"

—German proverb

LESSON 3

Gathering and Recording Information

A Strategies Lesson with Video

Looking Ahead

What This Lesson Is About

In this lesson, you will learn how important it is to have accurate information when you are trying to solve a problem, and you will practice techniques for gathering and recording information.

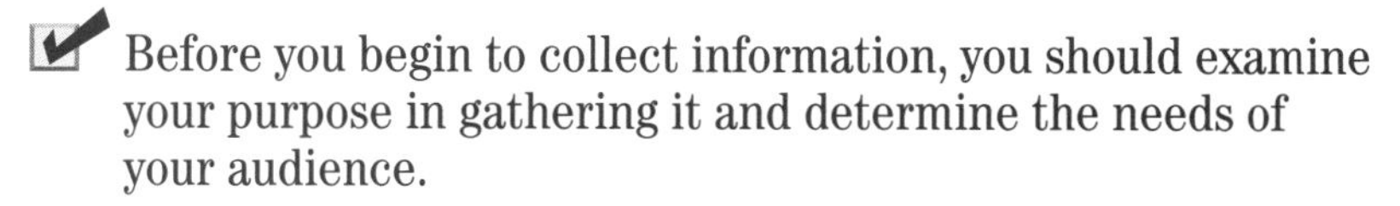

- ✔ Before you begin to collect information, you should examine your purpose in gathering it and determine the needs of your audience.

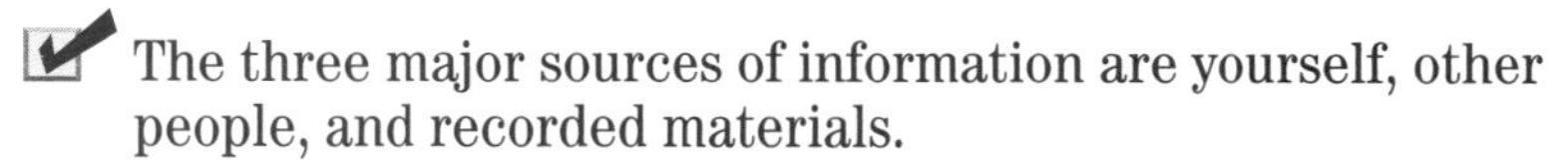

- ✔ The three major sources of information are yourself, other people, and recorded materials.
- ✔ The information you collect should be recorded in an organized form, such as a data matrix.

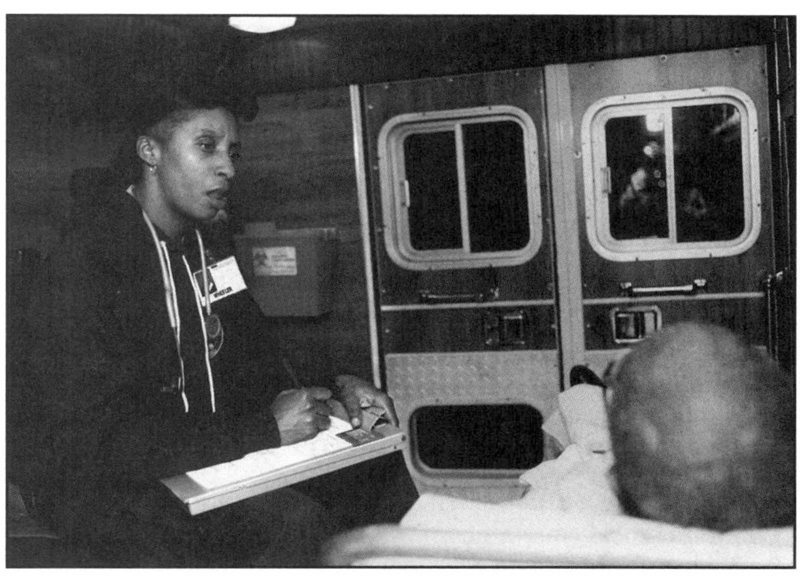

Paramedic Christy Wheeler of Grady Memorial Hospital in Atlanta, Georgia, uses a detailed form to gather and record information during 911 emergency calls.

Key Ideas

data matrix—a graphic device or table for recording information in a systematic way

relevant—related to, pertinent

reliable—dependable, trustworthy, authoritative

synthesize—combine various elements into a whole

timely—up-to-date, recent

What's for Supper?

Lauren has just returned from the supermarket. She lugs two bags of groceries into the kitchen, plops them on the table, and unpacks these items:

6 eggs	1 can water chestnuts
1 tomato	1 jar peanut butter
8 ounces spaghetti	1 bag shredded coconut
1 candy bar	1 pound hamburger
1 can hot chili beans	1 bag potato chips
1 onion	1 gallon milk
3 apples	1 green pepper

Suppose these are the only foods she has to make supper. Help her out by planning her menu. Be creative, but be careful—the list doesn't include any Alka-Seltzer, and you don't have to use all the ingredients in the same dish!

Be prepared to share your menu with the class.

Getting Started

Shopping for Information

Look at the list of Lauren's groceries again. If you wanted to make pizza for supper, would you have all the necessary ingredients? What if you were having company and two of your guests had special diets? If one of them were a vegetarian and the other could not eat any dairy products, how would their diets affect the ingredients you would use in your pizza?

Preparing a menu is not much different from gathering information for technical communication. In both cases, you should think about what you need and who your "audience" is before you start collecting your "ingredients." Otherwise, you may end up with a list like Lauren's—too much of some things, too little of others, none of some essential items, and a few odds and ends, such as the candy bar.

When you write a proposal—as you will in this module—you need information for three reasons:

To solve a problem—Learning more about the nature of a problem can help you come up with a reasonable solution. Even if you have a pretty good idea about what should be done to correct a problem, additional information can reassure you that you have a satisfactory solution, or it can point you in the direction of a better answer.

To enhance your credibility—If you can demonstrate that you know your subject well and if you can back up your argument with material from other sources, you will add to your own credibility. This is important in writing a proposal because your audience needs to feel sure that you know what you're talking about.

To write persuasively—Including reliable information to support your suggestion makes the proposal more persuasive. It helps you build a logical and compelling case that leads your reader to go along with your suggestion. Whether you are trying to get your boss to agree to a change in policy or asking an outside organization to provide funds for a special project, your writing must be persuasive.

The information you need must be on target: it must relate directly to your subject and must reflect the needs of your reader. As you begin gathering information, ask yourself two questions:

- **Who is my audience?** Who will read my proposal? What information do my readers need in order to make a reasonable decision—or to agree that my recommendation is the reasonable choice? What are my reader's concerns and priorities?
- **What is my purpose?** How will I use the information I gather? Do I want to inform my audience of their options, or do I want to persuade them to do something and to accept my recommendation for action?

Using what you have read, answer the following questions:

1 Why is it important to gather information to support your ideas?

2 What two questions should you ask as you begin your search for information?

Be prepared to share your answers with the class.

Sources of Information and Testing Information

Shopping for the information you need is a little more complicated than filling up a cart with pizza ingredients at the local supermarket. However, there are only three major sources of information: **yourself**, **other live sources**, and **recorded sources**.

Yourself as an information source. You may be an excellent source of information, especially if you have observed the problem firsthand. Or perhaps you have special knowledge that helps you understand why the problem occurred and how it may be solved. What do you know about the problem? Have you had special training related to it? Does a previous experience—at work, at home, with friends or family—relate in some way to the problem? If so, how? Before you seek information from other people and recorded sources, take a few minutes to ask yourself how much you already know. Think about how your knowledge and experience relate to the problem.

Other live sources. People who know about the problem, through either their professional expertise or their firsthand experience, can be another important information resource. If, for example, the problem you identified was homelessness, one good way to obtain information would be to talk to a sociologist or an economist who has published articles on that subject. Other good sources might be a homeless person or the director of a shelter. In general, information from other people is obtained through interviews. These may be conducted in person, on the telephone, or by mail or e-mail. Still another means of obtaining live information is through observation. For example, you could visit a shelter for the homeless, a food bank, or a soup kitchen and see what goes on there.

Recorded sources. These include print and electronic documents in libraries, on the Internet, and at governmental agencies. Start your search by exploring indexes, such as the *Reader's Guide to Periodical Literature*, and databases, such as the full-text newspaper articles available on CD NewsBank. Spend time exploring the Internet's general indexes—the search engines that provide lists of sites throughout the World Wide Web. Use the strategies outlined in the feature "Untangling the Web" (page 23) to guide your research efforts on the Internet.

On a Quest for Excellent Questions

Before you interview an expert, take time to create questions that will help the expert give you the information you need. Learn all you can about the topic, and then use the following tips to prepare your questions:

- Create questions that must be answered with a definition or an explanation. (How does this software program reduce errors in billing?)
- Follow yes/no questions with a question asking for further information. (Has the volume of customer calls increased? What factors have contributed to the increase?)
- Create questions that require a focused answer. (What specific strategies has your company used to increase recycling?)
- Divide complex questions into simpler questions. (Instead of "Describe the factors that contribute to homelessness and the strategies for addressing those factors," ask, "What factors contribute to homelessness?" Then follow up with, "What strategies could be used to address those factors?")
- Refer to the expert's work ("The article in the Sunday *Times* last month highlighted your efforts to help the local school district gain access to the Internet." "Your article on flextime in last week's *Business Weekly* supports the importance of listening to your employees.")

Always prepare more questions than you think you will need. When organizing your questions into an interview-question outline, group similar questions together.

You may also want to include in your outline brief notes on how you will introduce yourself and the topic to the expert before the interview and how you will thank the expert after the interview.

—Adapted from Rebecca E. Burnett, *Technical Communication*, 3d ed. (Belmont, CA: Wadsworth, 1994)

Untangling the Web

What do Yahoo, Excite! and Magellan have in common? Each one is a popular search database, or "engine," on the World Wide Web. Each will search the hundreds of thousands of Web sites in its database and create a list of sites that include whichever keyword(s) you enter in your request.

Selecting the right keyword or combination of keywords is necessary for a successful search. For example, if you want information on the Baltimore Orioles' Cal Ripken and enter the keyword "baseball," an engine would likely return a list of thousands of sites. Many of those wouldn't have any information on this ballplayer.

Here are several strategies you can use to untangle the web of related sites and find the information that you need:

- Link three or four keywords. Interested in classic motorcycles? Narrow your search by adding words that describe the information you seek, separated by the word "AND" (use capital letters). Enter your search as "motorcycles AND Harley-Davidson AND 1963" (but don't include the quotation marks). You'll be presented with sites that include all three words. With some search engines, you can type a plus sign (+) directly in front of a word that must be included in a site, instead of using "AND."
- Use quotes for phrases. If you're searching for information about a phrase or a name, such as "chicken quesadillas" or "Amy Grant," use quotation marks, as shown. Without them, most search engines will list any site that includes any one of the words in your phrase. Thus, your result list for the first example could include any Web site that used the word "chicken"; and your list for the second example, any site that included the word "grant." Enclosing the phrase in quotation marks will cause many search engines to return only those sites that include the phrase as written.
- Exclude keywords. Are your searches still yielding too many Web sites? Try excluding certain words by using the minus sign (–) or the word "NOT." If you don't know what to exclude, read several of the retrieved documents from your most recent search to see if there's a pattern. Let's say you're looking for fun places to go in Iowa, and you entered "Iowa AND entertainment." If your search turned up information for your least favorite recreation—fishing—run a more specific search. Try "Iowa +entertainment –fishing" or "Iowa AND entertainment NOT fishing." (Note that the plus and minus signs in the first example are typed as a part of the words they precede, without a space.) Either of these methods should eliminate the rod-and-reel sites.

—Adapted from Mary Kathleen Flynn, "Smarter Ways to Search the Web," *U.S. News & World Report* (June 10, 1996)

In gathering and recording information, it is important to be systematic. Here are some techniques that may prove helpful:

- To make sure you get the information you need, prepare questions before interviewing someone. Take notes during the interview. If the interviewee gives permission, you might want to tape-record the conversation as a backup for your notes.
- In conducting observations or site visits, use an observation sheet, sometimes called a data matrix (see the example on page 26). The matrix provides you with headings that prompt you to observe certain things that you need to know but might overlook.
- When you research recorded sources, you may find yourself faced with a number of long, technical documents to review. Learn to scan the documents, looking for guideposts that will help you determine whether the document is relevant to your needs. Look for keywords in the table of contents and index and in titles, subtitles, and summary statements. Also look at headings, subheadings, key sentences, illustrations, graphs, tables, and charts, as well as case studies that focus on the main points of the article.
- You can speed up your Internet searches by using a Web site's internal search engine to search for a key phrase. Your search will go faster if you turn off the images option on your World Wide Web browser. Focusing your search first on educational and governmental sites increases your chances of quickly finding reliable information. Look for WWW addresses that end with ".edu" and ".gov".

The information you collect can be recorded in different ways. It can be written on index cards, entered directly into the computer, or recorded on a data matrix. The data matrix—particularly helpful for recording observations—will be described in **Trying It Out**.

As you explore live and recorded sources, test the information you find against three criteria: **relevance**, **timeliness**, and **reliability**.

- **Is the information directly related to my topic?** If it isn't relevant, don't gather it or lose time reading it.
- **Is the information timely?** In most situations, it is important to use recent books, articles, and other sources to be sure that you have the results of the latest research and thinking.
- **Is the source reliable?** Be sure that your source does not have a conflict of interest—for example, a business reason for promoting one product over another. Government documents are usually reliable sources. So are authors with expertise in the field and people with firsthand knowledge of the problem.

Any Questions?

"Get to know what it is you don't know as fast as you can."

—Robert Heller, *The Super Manager*

"It is better to know some of the questions than all of the answers."

—James Thurber, American essayist, short-story writer, and humorist

"Asking the right questions takes as much skill as giving the right answers."

—Robert Half, *Robert Half on Hiring*

Using what you have read, answer the following questions:

1. What are three main sources of information?
2. What are at least three techniques for making information gathering and recording more systematic?
3. What three questions can be used to test the information you collect?

Be prepared to share your answers with the class.

Trying It Out

Viewing the Videodisc—Gathering Information

You are about to see a video segment in which the Channel 3 news staff gathers information on the training of entry-level employees and observes them at work. The employees use some of the information-gathering techniques you learned in **Getting Started**. As you watch, try to identify the various techniques they use.

Gathering Information

Search 26519, Play to 29766

Post-Viewing Activity

In the video, Carmen took you on a tour of the station to see employees at work. Use your copy of the **Observation Data Matrix** to record what you observed on the tour. You may need to view the segment several times to be sure that you have recorded all the information.

Be prepared to share your data matrix with the class. If necessary, add to your matrix any information that you missed during your observation. Keep your matrix handy for use in the next activity.

"The floor director is the link between the studio and the control room."

Activity Form

Observation Data Matrix

	Task 1	Task 2	Task 3	Task 4	Task 5
What is the task?					
What is the purpose of the task?					
What is involved in doing the task?					
What are the safety warnings, if any?					
Other observations:					

Summing Up

Pulling It Together

The e-mail responses Jack received when he queried the other technical directors appear on page 28. Anita's report on the current instructional materials is contained in her memo to Jack, which also appears on page 28. Use these materials and the data matrix that contains your observations to summarize the information you have gathered from your three sources. (Write one or two paragraphs to sum up what you have learned about the training of entry-level employees.) Use a heading to identify the main focus of each paragraph.

Be prepared to share your summary with the class for feedback. Keep it in your portfolio for use in other lessons of this module.

> ***"It's a healthy thing now and then to hang a question mark on the things you have long taken for granted."***
>
> —Bertrand Russell, English philosopher, mathematician, and social reformer

Keeping Track

On a separate sheet of paper, answer the following questions. Use what you have learned in this lesson to help you.

1. What two questions should you ask before starting to gather information?
2. What are the three main sources of information?
3. Why is it important to record the information you collect in an organized manner?

Channel ③

MEMO

TO: Jack Teller
FROM: Anita
DATE: May 4, ——
SUBJECT: Existing instructions for training entry-level employees

I searched through our files and asked existing employees for any instructions that could be used to train entry-level employees. The only thing I could find was the instructions for operating an earlier version of the Teleprompter. All I can say is that a person with an advanced degree in electronics engineering would have a hard time understanding them! What's more, they're handwritten and seem to be missing some steps. Suggestions for solving problems were scribbled in the margin next to the step where the problem might occur—very hard to read! Our instructions need to be accessible for our entry-level employees.

E-mail Responses

Date: Fri, 8 May —— 8:17 AM
From: "Antony Distasi" <tdistasi@qvtv.com>
To: "Jack Teller" <teller@TV3.com>
Subject: RE: training methods for entry-level employees

> 1. What tasks do your entry-level people do?

They run errands, they operate the Teleprompter, and they sometimes operate cameras.

> 2. How are they trained?

By mid-level employees or an entry-level employee who has been on the job more than six months. Person provides new employee with detailed written instructions and walks him through the process. We encourage cross-training so we always have someone who can step in if we're short-handed.

> 3. What are most effective ways of training entry-level employees?

You name it, we've tried it: sending new hires to workshops, cross-training with other employees, training manuals, even cooperative training with the local public access station. I think employees learn best when they have to work with the equipment as they learn, but with supervision. Also, our instructions are reviewed at least once a year to make sure they're up-to-date.

>Thanks!

Hey, you're welcome. Are we on for racquetball at the meeting this August? Best two out of three?

Tony

Date: Thu, 7 May —— 3:22 PM
From: "Lee Ann Ruslan" <laruslan@kntv.com>
To: "Jack Teller" <teller@TV3.com>
Subject: RE: training methods for entry-level employees

Hi Dave,

Our entry-level employees basically do the same things yours do. We have new hires shadow another entry-level employee on the job for a few weeks to make sure he knows the drill. We've tried seminar-type training, but this hands-on training works better for us. Unfortunately, we still have some problems with people knowing what to do.

Hope this helps.

Lee Ann

Going Further

- Gathering information and organizing that information are part of every occupation—and they can be two of the most valuable tools in your career-development toolbox. You'll gather and organize information when you apply and interview for jobs. You'll gather and organize information to do your job and to keep up on the latest developments in your profession. Get a head start on identifying the information sources you'll need by creating a handbook of resources in the occupational area that interests you. Look for live and print resources, and cast a wide net. Are there electronic resources? Local resources? Live resources within the profession? Take notes on the resources you identify, including such data as the title (or name), the location, the library call number, the World Wide Web address, and contact information. Include a brief description of what the source has and how its information may help you. Try to identify at least five sources in each of the two categories—print and live resources. Divide your notes according to these two categories, and organize your information in a way that makes your handbook easy to read and use. Be prepared to share your handbook with the class.

- How observant are you? Some occupations require a great deal of observation and close attention to detail—for example, fire investigators, police detectives, private investigators, and quality-control inspectors for industries such as pharmaceutical companies and meat-processing firms. Choose one of these occupations—or another one that requires excellent observation skills—and find out how someone in that job gathers and organizes information. Use a variety of live and recorded sources, and organize your information using notes or visual aids, such as photographs or diagrams. Then use what you've learned to write a short scenario on how you would solve a problem if you were that professional. For example, if you chose "fire investigator," then

An Inspector's Checklist

There are inspectors in nearly every occupational area, from agriculture to transportation:

- ✔ **Agricultural-chemicals inspectors** protect American agriculture by inspecting establishments where agricultural-service products are manufactured, sold, or used.
- ✔ **Aviation-safety inspectors** ensure that Federal Aviation Administration regulations that govern the quality and safety of aircraft equipment, operations, and personnel are maintained.
- ✔ **Bank examiners** investigate financial institutions to enforce federal and state laws and regulations governing the institution's operations and solvency.
- ✔ **Consumer-safety inspectors** inspect food, feeds and pesticides, weights and measures, biological products, cosmetics, drugs, and medical equipment, as well as radiation-emitting products.
- ✔ **Immigration inspectors** interview and examine people seeking to enter the United States and its territories.
- ✔ **Occupational safety and health inspectors** visit places of employment to detect unsafe machinery and equipment or unhealthy working conditions.
- ✔ **Postal inspectors** observe the functioning of the postal system and enforce laws and regulations.
- ✔ **Travel-accommodations raters** inspect hotels, motels, restaurants, campgrounds, and vacation resorts.

—Adapted from *Occupational Outlook Handbook* (1996–97 edition), U.S. Department of Labor (January 1996) use what you learned to write a story on how you would respond to a suspicious early-morning fire that gutted a downtown business. Be prepared to share your story with the class.

- Many hundreds of years ago, news was circulated by athletes who would run long distances—and sometimes for many days—to deliver their messages. Today, news is circulated through machines that deliver electronic signals almost instantly. In this lesson, you've gone behind the scenes with the production crew responsible for a weekend news broadcast. Use what you've learned about gathering and organizing information to identify five different sources for news. Analyze each source, and try to identify its strengths and its weaknesses as a news-delivery medium. Create a data matrix to help you gather and organize this information. Then choose the source you like the most and, if possible, bring an example of it to class. Be prepared to discuss the news sources and your choice with the class.

LESSON 4

Learning about Instructions

A Concept Lesson

Looking Ahead

What This Lesson Is About

In this lesson, you will learn about different kinds of instructions. You will also learn about the techniques that writers use to persuade people to read and use instructions. Then you will apply several criteria to judge the effectiveness of written instructions.

- Good instructions are written clearly and accurately and are arranged in chronological order.
- They are designed for a particular audience. To persuade people to follow them, the language, graphics, and overall design of the instructions reflect the needs, interests, and knowledge of the audience.
- Safety warnings in the instructions are clearly displayed at the points where injury is most likely to happen.

DAN DIDN'T BELIEVE IN FOLLOWING DIRECTIONS

Key Ideas

chronological—in the order of time, from first occurrence to last

pocket reminder—a brief list of key steps from a set of instructions; these steps are used to stimulate the memory of someone who knows how a process works but may need to be reminded

rationale—reason or justification for performing a task

Instructions—Who Needs Them?

Suppose you have ordered a piece of exercise equipment that you saw in a catalog. The catalog says, "Some assembly required," but when the equipment shows up at your door, you get five cartons, a bagful of nuts and bolts of varying sizes, and a 15-page instruction booklet. How would you react? Would you ship it all back to the company? Would you read the instructions and follow them step-by-step to assemble the device? Or would you ignore the instructions and try to put the machine together by using your instincts and the picture on the carton as a guide?

On a separate piece of paper, write what you would do and give the reasons for your decision. Then list a few reasons why some people might resist using the instructions. Also tell what the manufacturer could do to encourage people to use them.

Be prepared to share your responses with the class.

Getting Started

Instructions: The Long and the Short of It

Instructions come in all sizes. Some are as short as the six words on the top of an aspirin bottle: "To open, push down and turn." Others, such as technical manuals for complicated pieces of equipment, may run hundreds of pages long. No matter how long or complex they are, all instructions are meant to tell the reader how to solve a problem or how to do something. That "something" may be performing a task, operating or maintaining a piece of equipment, or following a process or procedure.

- **Performing a task.** A recipe for making lasagna, the directions for assembling a piece of furniture, and a list of steps for hooking up a VCR to a TV set are examples of instructions for performing a task.
- **Operating or maintaining a piece of equipment.** Directions for sending a fax or for pumping gas are common

examples of instructions for operating equipment. Routine maintenance instructions, such as those for adding toner to a copying machine, may be found in the user's manual; more complicated operations, such as replacing a major part or reprogramming default settings, may be covered in the technical manual.

- **Following a process or procedure.** Most companies have standard procedures for employees to follow. How to file grievances, how to handle orders, and how to request leave time are three examples of procedural or process instructions. Usually they appear in the personnel manual.

Most instructions combine verbal information with photos, diagrams, or other illustrations. The length of the instructions depends on the complexity of the subject matter and on the way people will use them. For example, a technical manual may provide extensive mechanical descriptions along with its instructions on how to complete a task. On the other hand, a pocket reminder, such as the sample below, may simply provide cues for someone who has learned a complicated procedure but could forget a key step.

The chart on the following page shows the advantages and disadvantages of various forms of instructions.

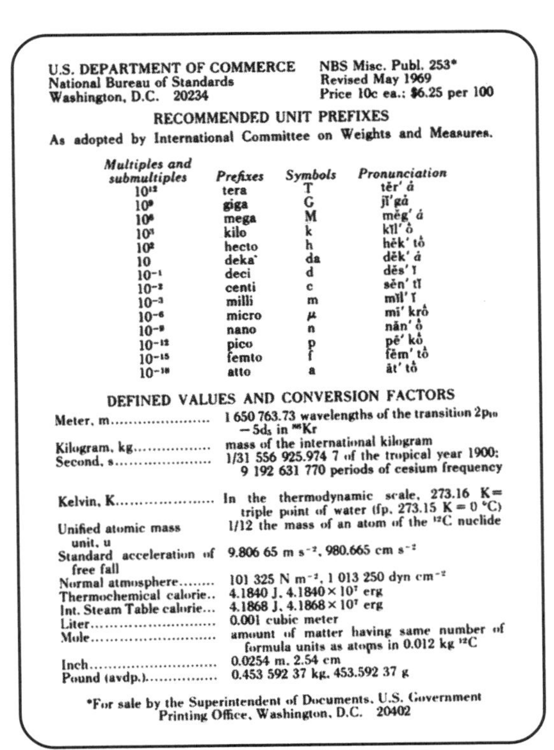

U.S. DEPARTMENT OF COMMERCE
National Bureau of Standards
Washington, D.C. 20234

NBS Misc. Publ. 253*
Revised May 1969
Price 10c ea.; $6.25 per 100

RECOMMENDED UNIT PREFIXES

As adopted by International Committee on Weights and Measures.

Multiples and submultiples	*Prefixes*	*Symbols*	*Pronunciation*
10^{12}	tera	T	tĕr′ ȧ
10^{9}	giga	G	jĭ′gȧ
10^{6}	mega	M	mĕg′ ȧ
10^{3}	kilo	k	kĭl′ ô
10^{2}	hecto	h	hĕk′ tô
10	deka	da	dĕk′ ȧ
10^{-1}	deci	d	dĕs′ ĭ
10^{-2}	centi	c	sĕn′ tĭ
10^{-3}	milli	m	mĭl′ ĭ
10^{-6}	micro	μ	mī′ krô
10^{-9}	nano	n	năn′ ô
10^{-12}	pico	p	pē′ kô
10^{-15}	femto	f	fĕm′ tô
10^{-18}	atto	a	ăt′ tô

DEFINED VALUES AND CONVERSION FACTORS

Meter, m	1 650 763.73 wavelengths of the transition $2p_{10} - 5d_5$ in ^{86}Kr
Kilogram, kg	mass of the international kilogram
Second, s	1/31 556 925.974 7 of the tropical year 1900; 9 192 631 770 periods of cesium frequency
Kelvin, K	In the thermodynamic scale, 273.16 K = triple point of water (fp. 273.15 K = 0 °C)
Unified atomic mass unit, u	1/12 the mass of an atom of the ^{12}C nuclide
Standard acceleration of free fall	9.806 65 m s^{-2}, 980.665 cm s^{-2}
Normal atmosphere	101 325 N m^{-2}, 1 013 250 dyn cm^{-2}
Thermochemical calorie	4.1840 J, 4.1840×10^7 erg
Int. Steam Table calorie	4.1868 J, 4.1868×10^7 erg
Liter	0.001 cubic meter
Mole	amount of matter having same number of formula units as atoms in 0.012 kg ^{12}C
Inch	0.0254 m, 2.54 cm
Pound (avdp.)	0.453 592 37 kg, 453.592 37 g

*For sale by the Superintendent of Documents, U.S. Government Printing Office, Washington, D.C. 20402

Front

GENERAL PHYSICAL CONSTANTS RECOMMENDED BY NAS–NRC Adopted by NBS[1]

Constant	Symbol	Value	Est.* error limit	Unit: Systeme Internat. (MKSA)		Unit: Centimeter-gram-second (CGS)	
Speed of light in vacuum	c	2.997925	3	$\times 10^{8}$	m s^{-1}	$\times 10^{10}$	cm s^{-1}
Elementary charge	e	1.60210	7	10^{-19}	C	10^{-20}	$cm^{1/2}g^{1/2}$†
		4.80298	20			10^{-10}	$cm^{3/2}g^{1/2}s^{-1}$‡
Avogadro constant	N_A	6.02252	28	10^{23}	mol^{-1}	10^{23}	mol^{-1}
Electron rest mass	m_e	9.1091	4	10^{-31}	kg	10^{-28}	g
Proton rest mass	m_p	1.67252	8	10^{-27}	kg	10^{-24}	g
Faraday constant	F	9.64870	16	10^{4}	C mol^{-1}	10^{3}	$cm^{1/2}g^{1/2}mol^{-1}$†
Planck constant	h	6.6256	5	10^{-34}	J s	10^{-27}	erg s
Fine structure constant	α	7.29720	10	10^{-3}		10^{-3}	
Charge to mass ratio for electron	e/m_e	1.758796	19	10^{11}	C kg^{-1}	10^{7}	$cm^{1/2}g^{-1/2}$†
		5.27274	6			10^{17}	$cm^{3/2}g^{-1/2}s^{-1}$‡
Rydberg constant	R_∞	1.0973731	3	10^{7}	m^{-1}	10^{5}	cm^{-1}
Gyromagnetic ratio of proton	γ	2.67519	2	10^{8}	rad $s^{-1}T^{-1}$	10^{4}	rad $s^{-1}G^{-1}$†
(Uncorrected for diamagnetism, H_2O)	γ'	2.67512	2	10^{8}	rad $s^{-1}T^{-1}$	10^{4}	rad $s^{-1}G^{-1}$†
Bohr magneton	μ_B	9.2732	6	10^{-24}	J T^{-1}	10^{-21}	erg G^{-1}†
Gas constant	R	8.3143	12	10^{0}	J $K^{-1}mol^{-1}$	10^{7}	erg $K^{-1}mol^{-1}$
Boltzmann constant	k	1.38054	18	10^{-23}	J K^{-1}	10^{-16}	erg K^{-1}
First radiation constant ($2\pi hc^2$)	c_1	3.7415	3	10^{-16}	W m^2	10^{-5}	erg cm^2s^{-1}
Second radiation constant	c_2	1.43879	19	10^{-2}	m K	10^{0}	cm K
Stefan-Boltzmann constant	σ	5.6697	29	10^{-8}	W $m^{-2}K^{-4}$	10^{-5}	erg $cm^{-2}s^{-1}K^{-4}$
Gravitational constant	G	6.670	15	10^{-11}	N m^2kg^{-2}	10^{-8}	dyn cm^2g^{-2}

*Based on 3 std. dev., applies to last digits in preceding col. †Electromagnetic syst. ‡Electrostatic syst. [1] Reprinted with revisions from NBS TNB, Oct. 1963.

☆ GPO : 1969 OI—335-540

Back

Pocket reminders can cover any topic—from insurance to car repair to health tips. This pocket reminder from the National Bureau of Standards, U.S. Department of Commerce, provides a handy list of information used by physicists and other scientists.

	Advantages	Disadvantages
Video training tape	• allows individual use at the employee's own pace • serves as a self-teaching tool • can be reviewed periodically	• is not convenient as an ongoing reference material • requires equipment to view
Manual	• may combine words with photos, diagrams, or other illustrations • contains complete information on all aspects of a task or piece of equipment • provides rationale for every step • may provide technical information on how a device operates • serves as a good basic reference material	• may be intimidating because of length and complexity • is not convenient to use on the job • is expensive to duplicate
Instruction sheet/ Brochure	• may combine words with photos, diagrams, or other illustrations • provides steps briefly, with little explanation • is easy and inexpensive to duplicate • may provide additional detail and rationale	• may easily be misplaced
Poster	• can be placed where needed • relies largely on graphics • can communicate across language barriers	• allows only limited explanation
Pocket reminder	• provides brief instructions • is easy to use • serves as a handy guide	• does not allow extensive explanations • may easily be misplaced • may be difficult to read if type is small

Using what you have read, answer the following questions on a separate sheet of paper.

1. What are instructions designed to do?
2. What are some common forms of instructions?
3. What two forms of instructions are best for employees who have learned how to perform a complicated procedure but may need a reminder to make sure they don't forget a step?

Be prepared to share your answers with the class.

Useful Instructions That Get Used

Instructions will not do any good if no one uses them. To be effective, instructions must persuade a reader to use them. Many people—perhaps you are one of them—resist following written instructions. Instead, they jump right in, relying on intuition and trial and error to assemble a piece of equipment or figure out how it works. This approach is inefficient. It leads to mistakes, and it wastes time. It can also be risky, because instructions often include safety warnings that are meant to keep people from injuring themselves or damaging the equipment.

Why do people resist reading instructions? Are they just too lazy? Not necessarily. People are influenced by their prior knowledge. They may be experienced with the task and not need instructions. In many cases, the instructions themselves are to blame. If the instructions are confusing, hard to follow, too long, or too complicated, people will feel overwhelmed. If the instructions look deadly dull—for example, if they contain large blocks of print with no subheads or graphics, or if the type is too small for easy reading—they will turn readers off.

Persuasive instructions—ones that are both useful and used—have the following characteristics:

- They are clearly identified by a title describing their use.
- They include a list of parts or equipment needed to complete the task.
- They list the steps in the order in which they are performed—that is, in chronological order. This makes the steps easier to follow and encourages the user to proceed in a logical manner.
- They use design elements such as white space, color, and variation in type size and font to increase their appeal and make reading easier.
- They provide the rationale for a step when knowing it will help the user perform the step more effectively, be more willing to perform it, or remember it for future use.
- They include any necessary warning signs and cautions at the point where these are needed.
- They are written in clear, concise language.
- They supply diagrams that are clear and accurate.

The directions on page 36 for replacing the dry-ink cartridge in a copying machine illustrate many of the characteristics of effective instructions.

Some instructions include detailed descriptions of the equipment's operating mechanism. Mechanical descriptions are discussed in Lesson 6. Lessons 8 and 9 explore design elements that make instructional materials more effective.

Using what you have read, answer the following questions. Use a separate sheet of paper.

4 In what order should the steps be given?

5 When should a rationale be included in a step?

3 What purpose do white space, color, and type size serve in instructions?

"Enormous blocks of print look formidable to a reader. He has a certain reluctance to tackle them; he can lose his way in them."

—William Strunk, Jr., and E. B. White, *The Elements of Style*

How to Replace Dry-Ink Cartridge in Models 5018, 5028, and 5034 Copiers

Title and easily identifiable purpose

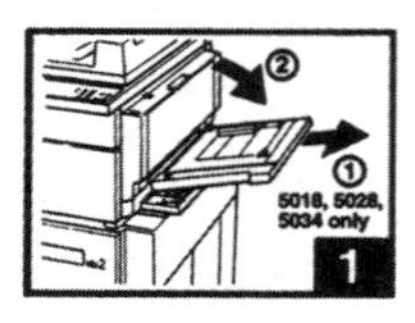

1. Remove tray (1) and open door (2).

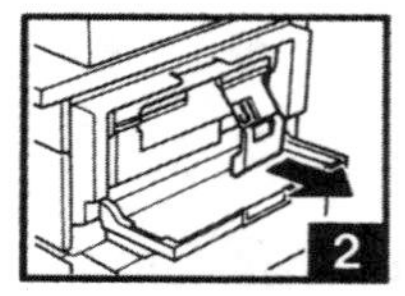

2. Grasp the lower J1 grip area of the catch tray and put it toward you.

Easy-to-read and accurate language

3. Using both hands on the green top edges, rotate the cartridge down until it stops.

Steps listed in chronological order

Readable font, inviting design

4. Using both hands on the green top edges, pull the cartridge toward you and out of the copier.

Accurate diagrams

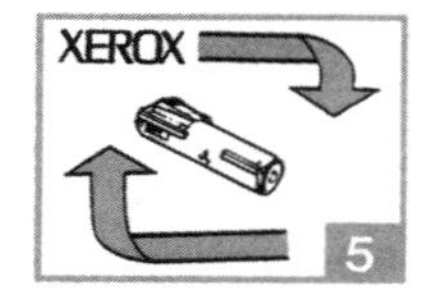

5. Put cartridge aside to return for recycling. **WARNING: Do not incinerate old cartridge.**

Clear warning at point of use

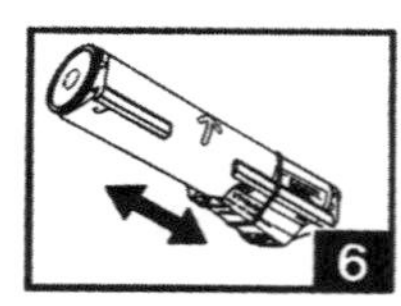

6. Remove new dry-ink cartridge from box. Hold it as shown and shake well. This will loosen the dry ink. Remove the rubber band.

Rationale given when it will motivate user or improve accuracy or precision

7. Using both hands on the green top edges, place the new cartridge in the copier. **CAUTION: Be sure the arrow is visible, as shown.**

Caution at point of use

8. Rotate the cartidge in the direction of the arrow until it stops and the green strip on the cartridge is aligned with the green strip on the developer module.

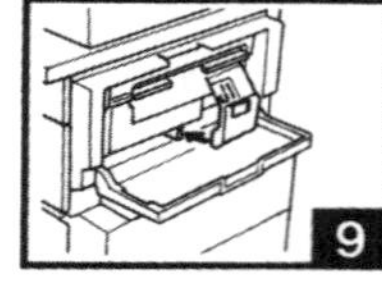

9. Slide the catch tray into position until it clicks.

10. Close the door (1) and install the tray (2)

Trying It Out

Do These Instructions Measure Up?

In **Getting Started**, you saw how the directions for changing a dry-ink cartridge in a copier incorporated many characteristics of good instructions. Those same characteristics can be used as criteria for measuring the effectiveness of other instructions.

Read the instructions in "To Relieve Choking (Clearing a Blocked Airway)" below. These instructions tell how to administer first aid to a person who has started to choke. Then evaluate the effectiveness of the instructions by filling out a copy of the **Instruction Assessment** form on page 38. For each "no" answer you give, either offer a suggestion for revising the directions to meet the criterion or explain why the element is not important for these instructions.

Be prepared to share your completed form with the class.

To Relieve Choking (Clearing a Blocked Airway)

If a person is choking but is able to cough forcefully and speak, encourage him or her to continue coughing. This may expel the object lodged in the airway.

If the person cannot cough or speak, the airway may be completely blocked and the person may not be getting enough air to stay alive. In this case, offer your assistance.

CAUTION: If the victim is conscious, be sure to get his or her permission to assist before you proceed.

1. Stand behind the victim and wrap your arms around his or her waist. Place the thumb side of one fist against the middle of the abdomen, just above the navel but below the rib cage.
2. Grasp the fist with the other hand.
3. Give quick, upward thrusts until the object is coughed up. **CAUTION: If the victim is visibly pregnant, give upward thrusts to the chest (in the center of the breast bone) rather than the abdomen.**
4. Take the victim to the emergency room to check for possible injuries even if normal breathing is restored.

Summing Up

Can You Fix These Fax Instructions?

The following office situation demonstrates the importance of clear, concise instructions. Read the story, and then follow the directions below.

> It's your first day on the job, and your supervisor stops at your desk to introduce you to the fax machine. "Sending a fax is a simple process," she says. "So why does everybody screw up? George sent out 20 blank pages this morning—and we're always having paper jams!" She waves a sheet of paper in the air. "Everybody received these instructions. I don't see why we're having so much trouble."

Instruction Assessment

Criteria	Yes	No	If "No," Suggested Improvement
1. Do the instructions have a clear title, and does the title explain the purpose of the instructions?			
2. Do the instructions include a list of parts or equipment needed to complete the task?			
3. Do the instructions identify the steps for completing the task in the order in which they are to be performed?			
4. Is the language clear, concise, and easy to understand? Is the reading level appropriate for the user?			
5. Are all text and accompanying diagrams accurate?			
6. Is the rationale for steps provided whenever necessary?			
7. Do the instructions use white space, color, and various type fonts effectively, thereby encouraging the reader to read them?			
8. Does the design make it easy to follow the instructions?			
9. Is a caution or warning given whenever the user will need such information?			
10. Is the user's prior knowledge taken into account in the instructions?			

11. What other form might be used to present these instructions?

12. What changes would be needed to adapt them to a different format?

She hands you the instruction sheet and storms back to her office. You pick it up and start reading:

> How to Send a Fax
>
> Never load more than 20 pages at one time. Make sure that all pages are on the same type of paper. Never send wet, wrinkled, curled, or folded sheets or pages held together by paper clips or staples. Be sure power is on. Place documents facedown in the document feeder. The "On Line" light should start blinking. Adjust the document guides to center the document in the feeder. If you have more than 20 pages, wait until some of the pages go through; then add the remaining pages to the top of those in the document feeder. If your original is very light, press the "Original" button once; if your document includes photographs, press the "Original" button twice (for "half-tone" setting). When the document is loaded and the "On Line" light is blinking, press the "Dial/Space" button. You will hear a dial tone. Use the numeric keypad to dial the fax number you are calling. If you make a mistake, press "Stop" and begin again. When the other fax machine answers, the "On Line" light will stop blinking, and your pages will begin to pass through the machine. If the line is busy, your fax machine will redial the number at three-minute intervals up to five times. If it is still busy after the fifth try, the "Alarm" light comes on and an alarm beep sounds for a few seconds. When a document is successfully transmitted, the message window shows the number of pages sent, and a long beep indicates that the operation is complete.

"No wonder there are problems," you say to yourself. "Who would want to read all this stuff?"

You decide to revise the instructions in a form that people will be more inclined to read—a form that will make the fax-sending process clear to everyone.

On a separate sheet of paper, revise the instructions. Use the criteria developed in this lesson to make the instructions user-friendly. If a diagram would help, either include it or describe how it should look.

Be prepared to compare your revised instructions with those of your classmates.

Keeping Track

On a separate sheet of paper, answer the following three questions. Use what you have learned in this lesson to help you.

1 Why are the steps in most instructions given in the order in which they are to be performed?

2. What are four characteristics of persuasive instructions?

3. Where should warnings and cautions appear in a set of instructions?

Going Further

- Locate three sets of instructions. You may find them at home, at school, in the library, or on the Internet. (For example, look for directions that tell how to operate a household appliance, how to change a tire, how to download a program on the Internet, or how to use an over-the-counter medication.) Photocopy or print out the directions, and use the criteria in this lesson to assess their effectiveness. Then write a memo to the manager of each firm that provided the instructions. In each of your memos, suggest some changes that would make the instructions more user-friendly and more helpful. Be prepared to turn in your instructions and memos.
- Imagine that you have been asked to adapt a set of instructions for users who have a very low reading level or who have trouble reading English. You are to create a poster or a reminder card that shows the main steps and that highlights any warnings or cautions. Choose a set of instructions from this lesson, and adapt it to your target audience. Be prepared to share your work with the class.
- Think of a process that you know well. Maybe it's cooking a favorite meal, going through an exercise routine, programming a VCR, creating a box within a text document on your computer, or tuning a musical instrument. Choose any task you have performed many times. Next, identify a group of people who would benefit by learning how to carry out the procedure. On a separate piece of paper, describe the general characteristics of this audience—age, gender, education or reading level, native language, and knowledge of the field. With the criteria for effective instructions in mind, create a set of instructions that would allow this audience to perform the procedure without difficulty and without risk. Don't forget to include any cautions or warnings related to the process. Be prepared to turn in your instructions to your teacher.

Simpler, More Concise Language

To reduce the information load contained in labels of over-the-counter drugs, the Food and Drug Administration proposes simplified wording. For example, three familiar warnings would be simplified to:

- "If pregnant or breast-feeding, ask a health professional before use" instead of "As with any drug, if you are pregnant or nursing a baby, seek the advice of a health professional before using this product."
- "Keep out of reach of children" instead of "Keep this and all drugs out of the reach of children."
- "In case of overdose, get medical help right away" instead of "In case of accidental overdose, seek professional assistance or contact a poison-control center immediately."

Also, the FDA proposes more than 35 simpler terms or phrases that can be used on the label instead of more complex or technical wording. For example, "lung" could be used instead of "pulmonary," and "help" or "aid" could be used instead of "assistance."

—Adapted from Dixie Farley, "Label Literacy for OTC Drugs," *FDA Consumer* (May–June 1997)

LESSON 5

Instructions for Destruction

A Literature Lesson

Looking Ahead

What This Lesson Is About

In this lesson, you will read an essay that is written as a set of instructions. It uses the literary forms of irony and satire to make an important point about the effect human beings have on the health of the planet.

- Writers sometimes find that it is effective to state the opposite of what they mean.
- Two techniques for stating the opposite of what you mean are irony and satire.
- To emphasize the importance of an issue to others, you can use irony and satire in giving written or oral instructions.

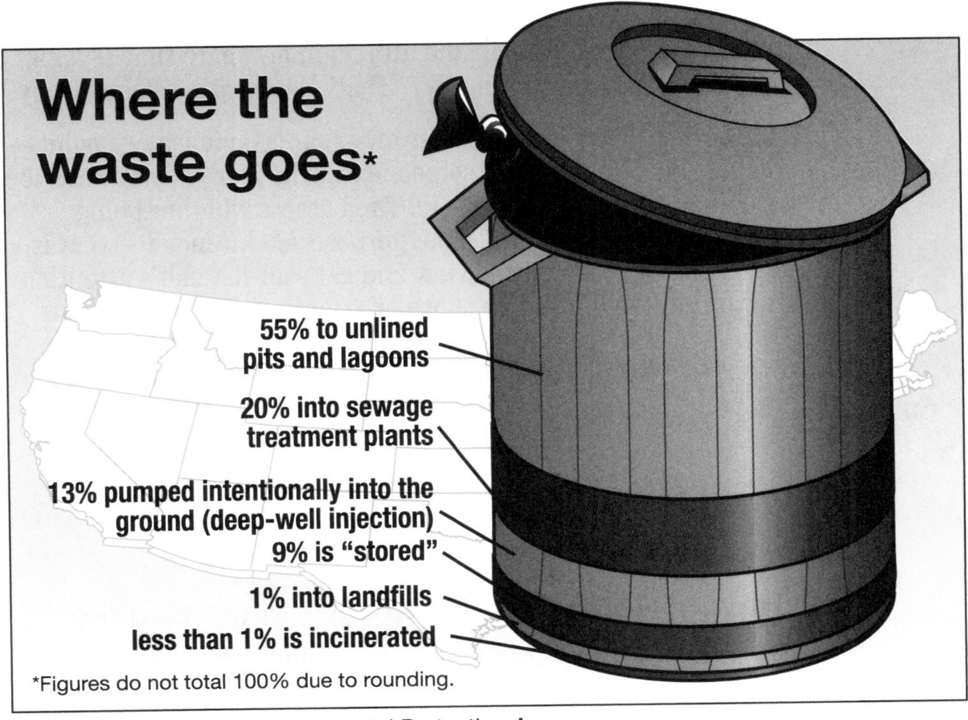

Source: United States Environmental Protection Agency

Key Ideas

irony—the use of words that say the opposite of what the speaker or writer means

sarcasm—irony that is deliberately harsh

satire—a literary work, usually delivered in a tone of irony, that makes fun of or scorns human foolishness or error

tone—the style or manner in which a person speaks or writes

Playing Off Opposites

Have you ever told a friend something that is, in effect, the very opposite of what you really mean? For example, suppose your friend accidentally betrays a secret—like letting it slip that you

> ***"Satire is a sort of glass, wherein beholders do generally discover everybody's face but their own."***
>
> —Jonathan Swift, English satirist

were at a party when you had told your girlfriend (or boyfriend) that you were home sick. You might respond, "Well, why don't you just tell it all? Why don't you say that I don't really have a job, either—that when I say I'm at work, I'm really out with someone else?" That's irony. You might even add: "Why don't you say that I'm just a big slob and all I do in my spare time is hang around the house watching TV?" That's sarcasm, or strong irony.

Think of a time when you used irony or sarcasm to make a point—with a friend, a teacher, or someone else. In your journal, describe the situation and what you said. Then assess whether being ironic or sarcastic achieved the purpose you intended—that is, to emphasize your point of view and get your listener's attention. Did you get the kind of response or attention that you wanted?

Be prepared to share your example with the class.

Getting Started

"How to Poison the Earth" by Linnea Saukko

One way to try to get people to do something is simply order them to do it. Giving an order works sometimes, but not always. Another way is to exhort people to do something. That means to incite them through strong arguments or warnings. You may occasionally be exhorted by your instructor.

There are also less direct means of persuasion. Speakers or writers may use satire and irony, mocking a situation or human condition they want fixed and saying just the opposite of what they mean.

©Jerry Bauer, provided by Alfred A. Knopf, Inc.

The essay you are about to read makes use of irony and satire. It was written by Linnea Saukko after she had spent three years developing programs to dispose of hazardous waste, a task that must have seemed overwhelming, given the amount of waste that Americans dump into the air, water, and land every day.

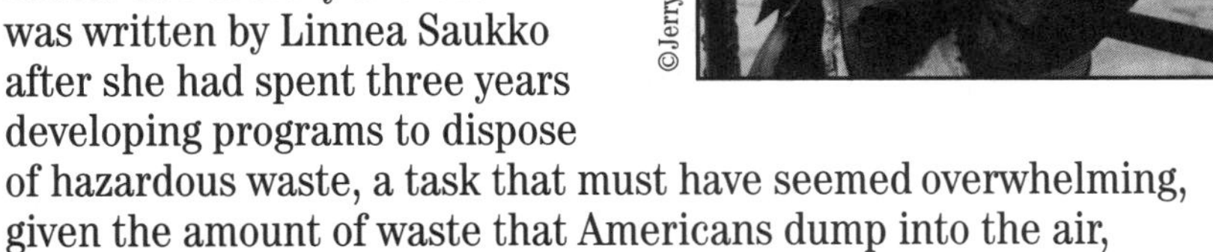

As you read the essay, list specific instructions the author gives for poisoning the earth.

Meet Linnea Saukko

Linnea Saukko wrote "How to Poison the Earth" as an assignment in a composition class at Ohio State University. It won a Bedford Prize in Student Writing and was published in *Student Writers at Work: The Bedford Prizes* (Nancy Sommers and Donald McQuade, eds. [New York: St. Martins, 1984]).

Born in Warren, Ohio, in 1956, Saukko earned a degree in environmental quality control from Muskingum Area Technical College. She then spent three years as an environmental technician. In this job she developed hazardous-waste programs and acted as an adviser on chemical safety at a large corporation.

When she became concerned about the lack of safe methods for disposing of hazardous waste, she went back to school to earn a bachelor's degree in geology (Ohio State, 1985) so that she could help address the issue. After graduation she went to work for the Ohio Environmental Protection Agency, where her duties included evaluating sites for possible groundwater contamination.

Literature Selection

How to Poison the Earth

Poisoning the earth can be difficult because the earth is always trying to cleanse and renew itself. Keeping this in mind, we should generate as much waste as possible from substances such as uranium-238, which has a half-life (the time it takes for half of the substance to decay) of one million years, or plutonium, which has a half-life of only 0.5 million years but is so toxic that if distributed evenly, ten pounds of it could kill every person on the earth. Because the United States generates about eighteen tons of plutonium per year, it is about the best substance for long-term poisoning of the earth. It would help if we would build more nuclear power plants because each one generates only 500 pounds of plutonium each year. Of course, we must include persistent toxic chemicals such as polychlorinated biphenyl (PCB) and dichlorodiphenyl trichloroethane (DDT) to make sure we have enough toxins to poison the earth from the core to the outer

generate—to originate, create, or cause

uranium-238—radioactive substance used to produce plutonium in nuclear reactors

plutonium—radioactive substance used to fuel nuclear reactors

toxic—poisonous

nuclear—pertaining to or powered by atomic energy

polychlorinated biphenyl (PCB)—a highly toxic industrial compound thought to cause cancer

dichlorodiphenyl trichloroethane (DDT)—a toxic compound used as an insecticide

toxin—a poisonous substance

core—the earth's innermost part, believed to be mainly solid iron and nickel

atmosphere—the air and gases that surround the earth

atmosphere. First, we must develop many different ways of putting the waste from these nuclear and chemical substances in, on, and around the earth.

With deep-well injection we can ensure that the earth is poisoned all the way to the core.

Putting these substances in the earth is a most important step in the poisoning process. With deep-well injection we can ensure that the earth is poisoned all the way to the core. Deep-well injection involves drilling a hole that is a few thousand feet deep and injecting toxic substances at extremely high pressures so they will penetrate deep into the earth. According to the Environmental Protection Agency (EPA), there are about 360 such deep injection wells in the United States. We cannot forget the groundwater aquifers that are closer to the surface. These must also be contaminated. This is easily done by shallow-well injection, which operates on the same principle as deep-well injection, only closer to the surface. The groundwater that has been injected with toxins will spread contamination beneath the earth. The EPA estimates that there are approximately 500,000 shallow injection wells in the United States.

Environmental Protection Agency (EPA)—the government agency charged with protecting the atmosphere, water, land, and people from dangerous pollutants

aquifer—a natural formation of rock, gravel, or sand that holds water underground and supplies it to wells and springs

contaminated—impure, unclean, or poisoned

lagoon—a pool for storing and treating human waste

Burying the toxins in the earth is the next best method. The toxins from landfills, dumps, and lagoons slowly seep into the earth, guaranteeing that contamination will last a long time. Because the EPA estimates there are only about 50,000 of these dumps in the United States, they should be located in areas where they will leak to the surrounding ground and surface water.

. . . use the ocean as a dumping place for as many toxins as possible.

pesticide—a chemical that kills plant or animal pests

Applying pesticides and other poisons on the earth is another part of the poisoning process. This is good for coating the earth's surface so that the poisons will be absorbed by plants, will seep into the ground, and will run off into surface water.

Surface water is very important to contaminate because it will transport the poisons to places that cannot be contaminated directly. Lakes are good for long-term storage of pollutants while they release some of their contamination to rivers. The only trouble with rivers is that they act as a natural cleansing system for the earth. No matter how much poison is dumped into them, they will try to transport it away to reach the ocean eventually.

Art by Maureen Pesta

The ocean is very hard to contaminate because it has such a large volume and a natural buffering capacity that tends to neutralize some of the contamination. So in addition to the pollution from rivers, we must use the ocean as a dumping place for as many toxins as possible. The ocean currents will help transport the pollution to places that cannot otherwise be reached.

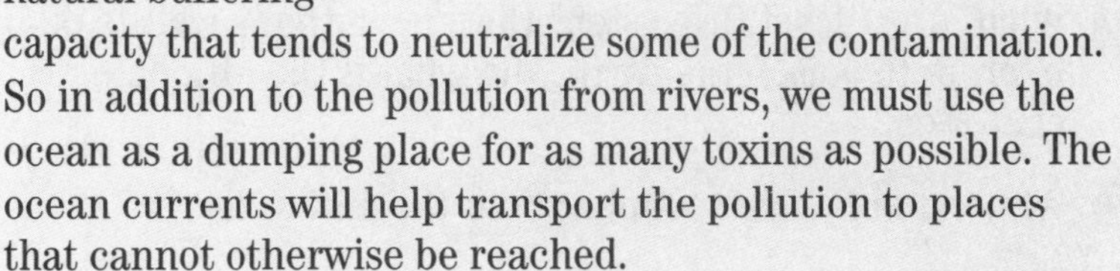

pollutant—a substance that poisons the air, water, or earth

buffering—shielding from harm

neutralize—to make something ineffective

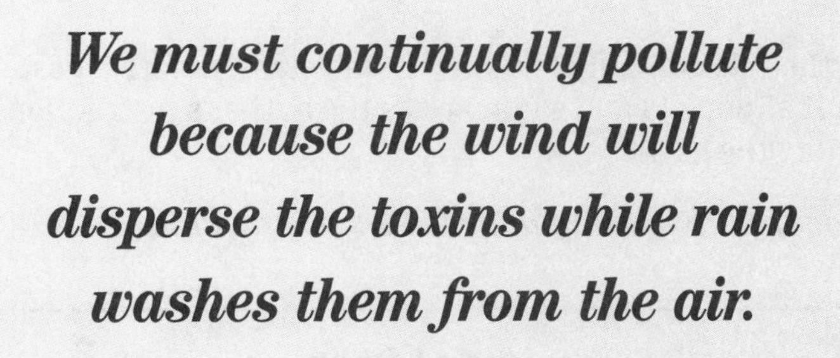

We must continually pollute because the wind will disperse the toxins while rain washes them from the air.

Now make sure that the air around the earth is very polluted. Combustion and evaporation are major mechanisms for doing this. We must continuously pollute because the wind will disperse the toxins while rain washes them from the air. But this is good because a few lakes are stripped of all living animals each year from acid rain. Because the lower atmosphere can cleanse itself fairly easily, we must explode nuclear tests bombs that shoot radioactive particles high into the upper atmosphere where they will circle the earth for years. Gravity must pull some of the particles to earth, so we must continue exploding these bombs.

combustion—the act of burning

evaporation—the process whereby water on the earth's surface is converted to water vapor in the atmosphere

acid rain—rainfall that contains industrial pollutants

radioactive particles—tiny airborne substances that emit harmful radiation

So it is that easy. Just be sure to generate as many poisonous substances as possible and be sure they are distributed in, on, and around the entire earth at a greater rate than it can cleanse itself. By following these easy steps we can guarantee the poisoning of the earth.

Trying It Out

Responding to "How to Poison the Earth"

Now that you have read the essay, answer the following questions. Support your answers with evidence from the reading. Record your responses on a separate sheet of paper.

1. What was your first clue that the essay was a satire written in a tone of irony?
2. What are some human practices that the author, through her irony, suggests are poisoning the earth?
3. What was the author's purpose in writing such a satirical essay?
4. What audience was the author targeting?
5. Is the purpose of the instructions clear? What is the purpose?
6. What are at least three steps that the author suggests taking in order to poison the earth, and what is the rationale for each step?
7. What equipment or supplies does the author list?

Be prepared to discuss your answers with the class.

Using the information contained in the essay, create a poster or mural that depicts and summarizes the author's instructions for poisoning the earth.

Be prepared to display your poster or mural in class.

Images of Satire

In this lesson, satire is presented in a written form, but satire also appears in other art forms, such as music and art. One form of satire is caricature. A caricature is a cartoonlike picture of a person, in which certain features or mannerisms are exaggerated for satirical effect.

Jack Nicholson, American actor

Another form is the comic strip, which can combine elements of caricature and written satire. American comic-strip artists Walt Kelly, Al Capp, Scott Adams, and Garry Trudeau are famous for their satire.

Reversing the Irony

Not all authors seeking to condemn the human folly of carelessly and dangerously creating and disposing of waste would approach it through satire. It would be possible to use the same information that Linnea Saukko presents to write a straightforward list of ways to *prevent* the poisoning of the earth.

Using the list that you made while reading Saukko's essay, prepare instructions for keeping the earth as healthy as possible. To do this, it may be necessary to state the opposite of what Saukko writes. For example, while Saukko states that "we should generate as much waste as possible from substances such as uranium-238," you might write, "We should generate as *little* waste as possible" from such substances. Write your instructions on a separate sheet of paper.

Be prepared to read and discuss your instructions in class.

Thoughts on the Environment

The maltreatment of the natural world and its impoverishment leads to the impoverishment of the human soul. It is related to the outburst of violence in human society. To save the natural world today means to save what is human in humanity.

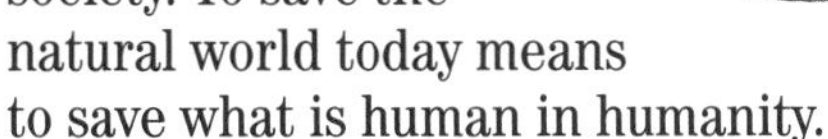

—Raisa M. Gorbachev, Russian political figure

Every person who builds a second home on a pristine lake or in a secluded area of woods, or who invests in urban-sprawl development, is part of the same global pattern of encroachment that displaces wildlife and decreases the wild space our own species needs for its survival.

—Deane Morrison, American science writer

The sea is the universal sewer.

—Jacques Cousteau, underwater explorer and filmmaker

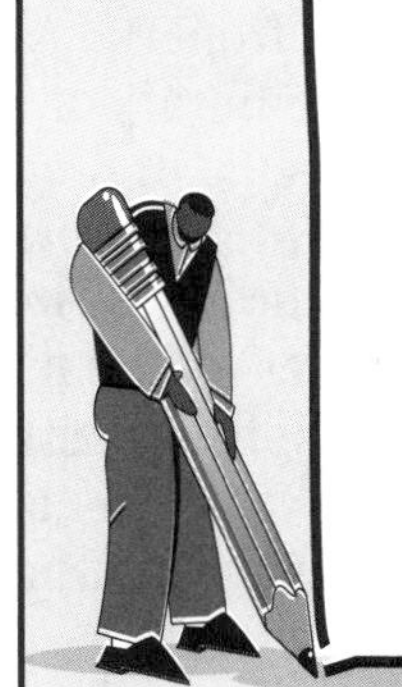

Summing Up

Writing Satire

We are often subjected to lectures and essays on serious topics: why we should stop smoking, exercise more, and avoid saturated fats in our diets. We are given reasons why we should vote in every election or donate blood during the next blood drive. Even though the evidence is strong in each case—even frightening in the statistics linking cancer with tobacco, heart attacks with high cholesterol—many people ignore this advice. Perhaps a satirical approach, like the one Linnea Saukko used, would be more effective.

Using what you have learned about irony, write a short satirical lecture or essay that urges people to smoke, to use drugs and alcohol, to become "couch potatoes," or to eat junk foods that are high in fat and cholesterol. Or use your satire to discourage people from voting or from giving blood. Remember that your *real* intent is the opposite of your stated intent—and that the evidence you give should support your real intent, even though it is used to justify the negative behaviors you are recommending.

Be prepared to share your work with the class.

Keeping Track

On a separate piece of paper, answer the following questions. Use what you have learned in this lesson to help you.

1. Why do some writers say the opposite of what they mean?
2. What are two techniques used by these writers?
3. Why are these two techniques sometimes useful in giving written or oral instructions?

Satire on the Web

The "Daily Muse" Web site provides satirical coverage of current news events (http://www.cais.com/aschnedr/muse.htm).

Going Further

- Satire is a literary form that has been used in many world cultures, from the early Greeks to contemporary Americans. Visit your library or go on-line and look up *satire* in a general encyclopedia or dictionary of literature, such as *Grolier's Encyclopedia*, *The Columbia Encyclopedia*, *A Handbook to Literature*, or *The Cambridge Guide to Literature in English*. Take notes on the history of satire. Then write a short essay telling aspiring writers about how satire has been written in Athens, Rome, England, and the United States. Be prepared to share your instructions with the class.

- Perhaps the most famous—or infamous—satire ever written is *A Modest Proposal* by Jonathan Swift (1667–1745). In this essay Swift savagely ridicules the English for their harsh treatment of the Irish. His "modest proposal," if it weren't satire, could be considered one of the most outrageous suggestions ever made for solving a social problem. Using whatever resources you can think of, find out what Swift's "modest proposal" is and write a brief explanation of it. Be prepared to hand in your explanation to your teacher.

- Watch a satirical TV show (or view a past show on videocassette). Write a brief essay describing ways in which the comedians use satire in their sketches. Be prepared to hand in your essay to your teacher.

LESSON 6

Creating Instructions

A Strategies Lesson with Video

Looking Ahead

What This Lesson Is About

In this lesson, you will learn how to write coherent and useful instructions. You will practice that skill by creating instructions for operating a Teleprompter and describing the way it works.

- ✔ Planning instructions involves analyzing both the audience and the task.
- ✔ Good instructions use the active voice, the imperative mood, and parallel construction.
- ✔ When instructions deal with operating a machine, they often include a description of the machine and how it works.

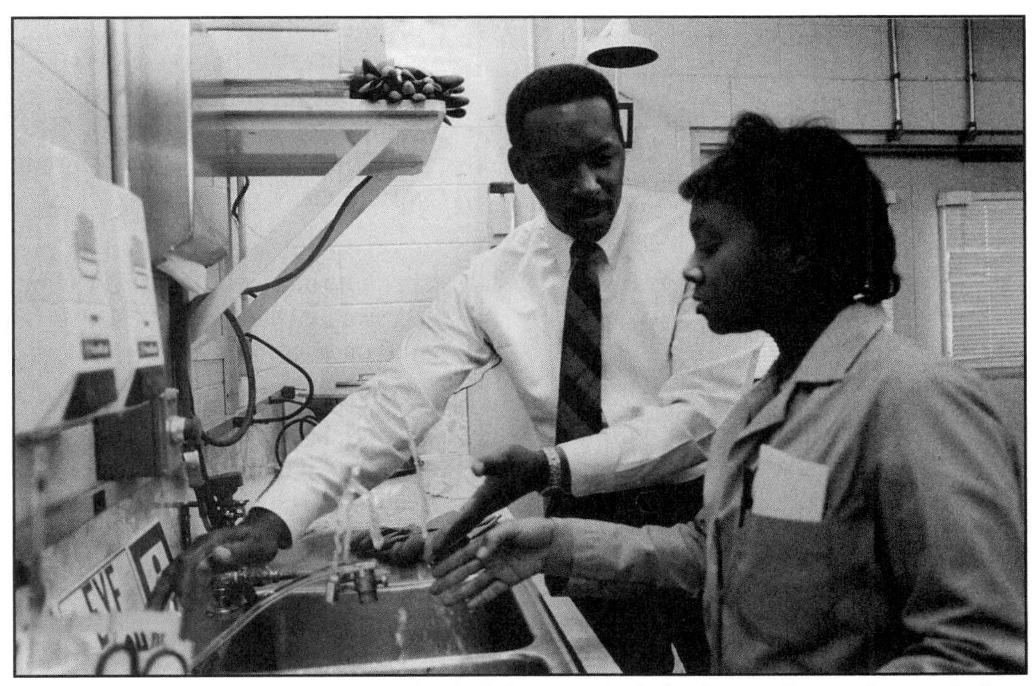

Rachelle's orientation to her new job in the laboratory includes instructions on how and when to use the eyewash fixture.

Key Ideas

active voice—sentence structure in which the subject performs the action

caution—indication of potential conditions that could damage the equipment or injure the operator

flowchart—a diagram showing the progress of a process in sequential order

imperative mood—sentence structure in which the reader or listener is commanded to do something

parallel construction—the use of the same grammatical structure in a series of related statements

warning—indication of potential hazards that may cause serious injury or death

Ball-Type Faucet Repair

1. Shut off water-supply valves, then drain lines by turning faucet on.
2. Use an allen wrench to loosen the set screw holding the handle in place, and remove handle.
3. Loosen and remove the adjusting ring by using the special wrench provided in the repair kit.
4. To remove cap, use pliers and turn counter-clockwise. Protect cap finish with cloth.
5. Remove spout assembly.
6. Remove cam assembly by pulling up on ball shaft. You may need to use pliers.
7. Removing seats and springs is best done by inserting a pencil or sharp tool into the seat assembly and gently lifting it out. Check and clean inlet ports before replacing seats and springs.
8. To replace "O" rings on body, use a sharp tool to pry away from body. Roll new correct size "O" ring into place.
9. When reassembling, be sure to align slot in ball with pin in body, and key on cam with slot in body.
10. Hand-tighten the cap, then screw adjusting ring into place with special wrench and replace handle. Turn on water and check for leaks. If necessary, further tighten adjusting ring.

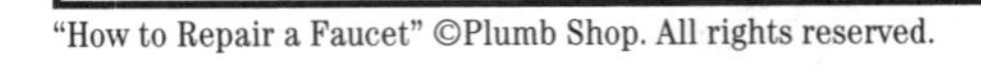

Can You Give Instructions?

Think of something that you know how to do well. For example, it might be making a special recipe handed down from your grandmother, changing a car's tires, diapering a baby. Pick a task that is familiar to you. On a separate piece of paper, write the instructions for performing that task. (For an example, see the instructions for repairing a ball-type faucet at left.) Assume that the person who will attempt to perform it has never done anything like this before. He or she must depend entirely on your instructions.

As you create your instructions, be sure that they meet the criteria for effective instructions. These are listed on page 35 of Lesson 4.

When you complete your instructions, exchange papers with another student. Imagine that you are to perform the task your partner has outlined. Could you do it with only the instructions you have been given? If not, what is missing?

Exchange suggestions with your partner on how the instructions could be improved, and keep the suggestions and your instructions for use later in this lesson.

Getting Started

Creating Instructions

As you may have discovered in the first activity in this lesson, creating your own instructions can be more difficult than evaluating someone else's. You need to know your audience—the people who are expected to use your instructions. You also need to know the task so well that you can break it down into the steps required to accomplish it. A flowchart can be a useful tool for analyzing the task. You also need to help the user get organized for the task.

Knowing your audience. Good instructions tell users what they need to know in terms that they will understand. The quickest way to discourage people from reading your instructions is to overestimate or underestimate their knowledge.

- If you assume that they know more than they do, you may leave out important steps or use terms that aren't clear. This can confuse the users and cause them to become discouraged when they fail to carry out the task.
- If you assume that your readers know nothing, you may insult and bore them by providing long explanations of processes with which they are already familiar.
- You should also consider whether your readers are fluent in English and whether they have disabilities (impairment of vision or hearing or a low level of literacy) that may interfere with their ability to understand the instructions.

Before you begin to create instructions, try to picture your audience—the people who will read and use them.

Analyzing the task. Regardless of who your users will be, the task remains the same: to create instructions that will ensure that the task is completed correctly. To accomplish this, you need to

- break down the task into separate steps.
- arrange the steps in the order they should be performed.
- identify any possible problems or safety hazards that might occur in the process of completing the task.
- consider any prior knowledge the user may have about the task.

Warnings and Cautions

Product liability laws provide monetary compensation for harm caused by a defective product. A manufacturer can be held responsible for any number of causes, including faulty packaging. Or the defect may come from failure to provide either adequate directions or appropriate cautions or warnings.

When you prepare instructions, you need to be sure that they satisfy the "legal requirements for adequacy." To do so, you need to

- understand the product and its likely users.
- describe the product's functions and limitations.
- fully instruct on all aspects of product ownership.
- provide clear, correct, and tested instructions.
- use words and graphics that suit the intended audience.
- appropriately warn of product hazards.
- offset claims of product safety in advertising or other materials with intense warnings. (If the advertising downplays dangers, you must be especially careful to include warnings to counter these promotional claims.)
- present important directions or warnings so that consumers can spot and follow them.
- meet government, industry, and company standards.
- reach product users. (You need to consider the best way to get the instructions to the user: In a package insert? In a separate manual?)
- inform consumers in a timely manner of defects discovered after marketing.

—Adapted from Rebecca E. Burnett, *Technical Communication*, 3d ed. (Belmont, CA: Wadsworth, 1994)

To help the user get organized, you also need to

- note any materials or tools that may be needed to complete the task.
- identify any special information that the user may need to know about the process or the equipment.

A flowchart is a helpful tool for analyzing the task. A simple flowchart can be similar to the one below: a series of boxes connected with arrows, in which you can list the steps in chronological order.

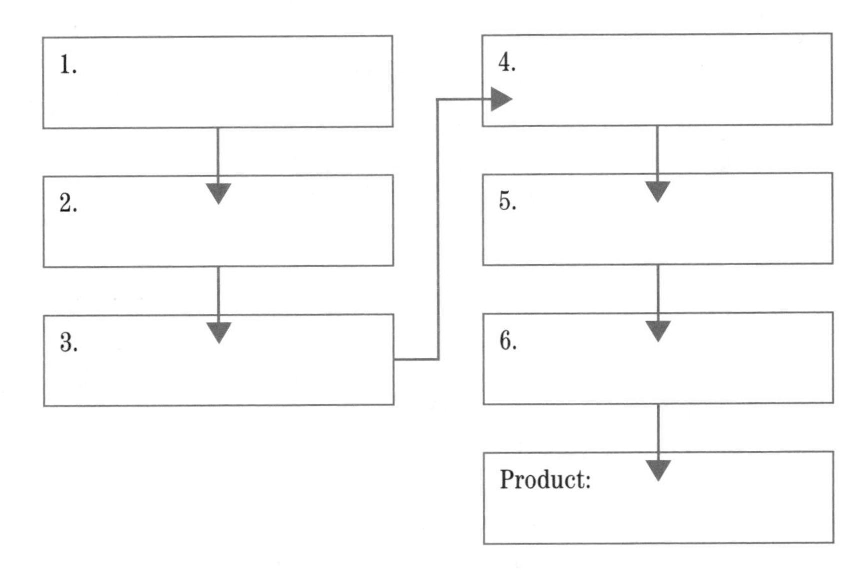

As you analyze your task, you may find that there are points at which the user must make choices and other points at which you will need to insert additional information, cautions, or warnings. These can be incorporated in the flowchart. The flowchart at the top of the next page, which shows the steps to take in clearing an error message from a fax machine, is an example of a more complex flowchart.

Using what you have read, answer the following questions:

1 Why is it important to know the audience for your instructions?

2 What operations should you perform to analyze the task?

3 How can a flowchart help you plan your instructions?

Be prepared to share your answers with the class.

Writing Instructions

As you choose the wording for the steps in your instructions, remember that your first aim is to communicate clearly and simply to the user. You want your instructions to be useful and used.

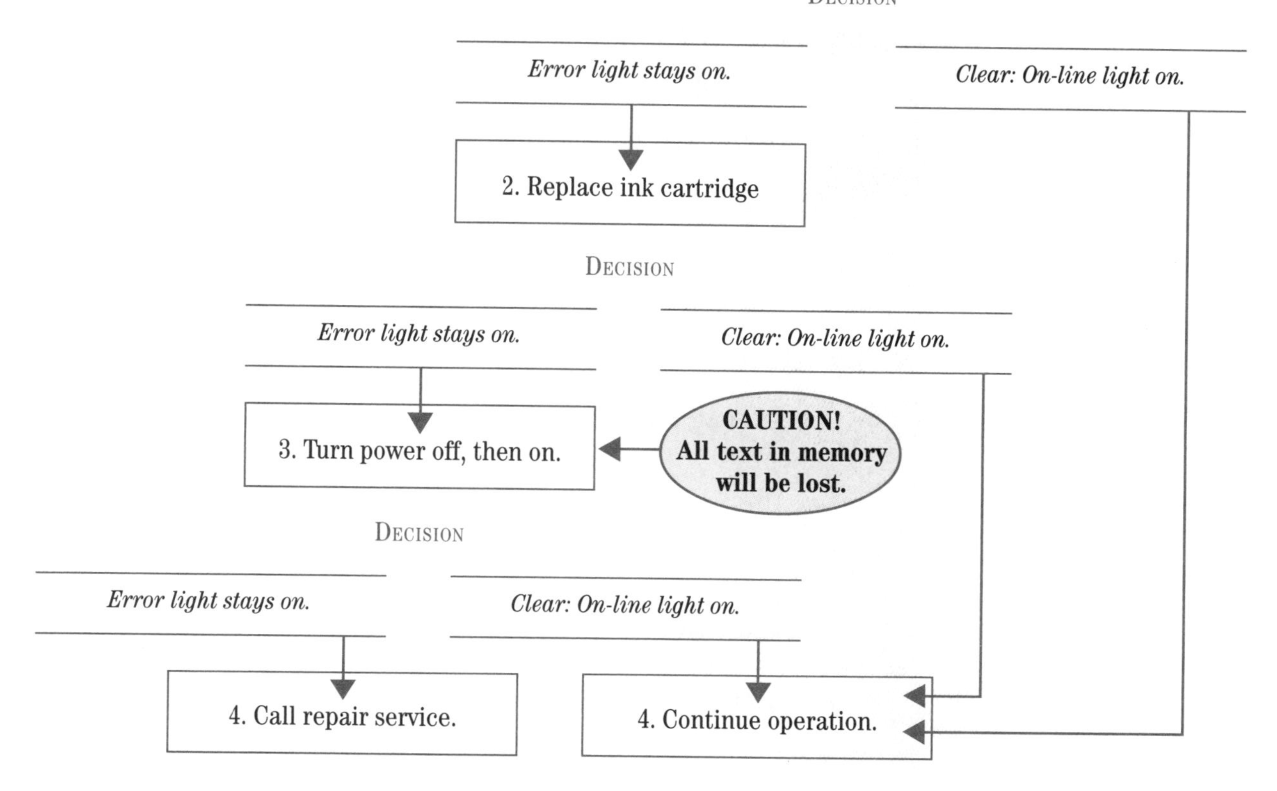

Four basic rules will help you do this:

1. **Keep your sentences short.** Break longer sentences into simple, short ones.

   Instead of: *"After opening the document feeder door, pull the ink cartridge down and remove it, being careful not to touch the metallic strip at the bottom."*

   Use: *"Open document feeder door. Pull down cartridge to remove it. Caution: Do not touch the metallic strip on the cartridge bottom."*

2. **Limit each step to one instruction.** Don't crowd several ideas into one step.

   Instead of: *"To find the cause of the error message, refill paper tray, replace ink cartridge, and turn power off and then on again."*

   Use: *"To find the cause of the error message:*

   1. *Refill paper tray.*
   2. *If light is still on, replace ink cartridge.*
   3. *If light is still on, turn power off and then on again.*
   4. *If light remains on, call service.*

3. **Make all the steps parallel in sentence structure.** Use complete sentences rather than phrases or "labels."

   Instead of: *"Proper tools"*

   Use: *"Have a Phillips screwdriver and a flashlight at hand."*

   Instead of: *"Other problems"*

   Use: *"Ask other employees to report difficulties."*

4. **Use the active voice and the imperative mood.** Instructions should be straightforward and forceful. In the active voice, the subject (the actor) precedes the verb (the action), and it is clear who performs the task. The imperative mood is used for commands or instructions. In an imperative sentence, the subject "you" is implied: "(You) Replace the cartridge."

   Instead of: *"The paper tray should be filled daily."* (passive voice)

   Use: *"Users should fill the paper tray daily."* (active voice)

   Instead of: *"The ink cartridge needs to be replaced."* (indicative mood)

   Use: *"Replace the ink cartridge."* (imperative mood)

Be prepared to discuss these rules with the class.

Mechanism Descriptions

Often instructions for operating a piece of equipment include a description of the equipment and how it works. This description provides a verbal (and sometimes a graphic) picture of the mechanism, states its purpose, lists and describes its parts, and details the function of each part.

To create a mechanism description, imagine that you are describing the device to someone who cannot see it (a person on the telephone, for example). Decide which elements of the mechanism are important to the person who will be using it. Then use the following general outline to develop your description.

- Give a general description of the mechanism, including the purpose for which it is used, and list its main parts.
- Describe each part under separate headings, such as size, shape, color, and composition. Also describe the function of each part.
- Provide a drawing of the mechanism.

Mechanism descriptions do *not* include directions for operating the device. These directions are part of your overall instructions for completing a task that involves the use of the mechanism.

Read the following mechanism description for a can opener. As you read, think about whether it follows the guidelines just stated.

Verb Vitality

Use active verbs whenever possible. The active voice will give your writing a drive and vigor that passive construction would destroy. Look at your newspaper for examples of active-voice writing: "The report praises the Clinton administration for increased funding for AIDS" and "The low overhead persuades many retailers to try temporary leasing." Experienced writers addressing themselves to millions of readers know that they have to be lively, forceful, and direct if they want to hold their audience. Without exception, these writers prefer the active voice.

—Ernst Jacobi, *Writing at Work* (Berkeley, CA: Ten Speed Press, 1985)

Hand-Held Can Opener

A hand-held can opener is used to open standard aluminum and tin cans in which food is stored. It will open cans with a shallow lip around the rim. This model will not open cans with smooth rims, such as soda-pop cans.

The hand-held can opener (see Figure 1) consists of the following parts: handle, blade and gear, and turning knob.

Handle

The handle consists of two 3-inch stainless steel moveable prongs that extend beyond the cutting mechanism. Each prong is encased in a smooth, $2\frac{1}{2}$-inch black plastic sheath to protect it from rust and to make it easier to grip. The prongs of the handle are pressed together by the user's hand to place the blades over the lip of the top of the can and to pierce the top of the can.

Figure 1

Blade

The blade, opposite the gear, is a $\frac{1}{2}$-inch diameter circle, about the size of a penny and made of gray metal. The outer edge of the circle is sharp, allowing the blade to cut the lid off the can.

Gear

The gear, located directly under the turning knob, is on the back of the opener. Approximately $\frac{1}{2}$-inch in diameter, or the size of a penny, it is made of stainless steel. Attached to the turning knob, the gear is placed under the lip of the can to grip the can.

Turning Knob

The turning knob is a $2\frac{1}{2}$-inch-long rectangular lever used to move the blade along the outer edges of the can. Located on the side opposite the blade and gear, it is made of stainless steel. The user turns the knob which, in turn, rotates the blade.

Using what you have read, answer the following questions:

1 What information is usually included in a mechanism description?

2 What information is not included in a mechanism description?

Be prepared to share your answers with the class.

Trying It Out

Viewing the Videodisc—Operating a Teleprompter

The entry-level employees at Channel 3 have some learning to do, and one area in which they desperately need instruction is in the operation of the old, backup Teleprompter. Your assignment will be to develop clear, concise, and complete instructions for these employees, along with a description of the backup Teleprompter mechanism. The instructions and mechanism description will be included in a proposal to the operations manager to enhance the training and training materials available to new employees.

Operating a Teleprompter

Search 29769, Play to 35456

You are about to see a video segment that describes the backup Teleprompter and tells how it works. As you watch, take note of the steps involved in using the old equipment. Pay special attention to any warnings or cautions that are needed. Also take notes for a mechanism description to be included in your instructions.

Post-Viewing Activity

You are now ready to create instructions for operating a Teleprompter. Here are some guidelines to follow:

- Using a copy of the **Planning Flowchart** on page 57, fill in the steps. Use one box for each step, and number the steps in the order in which they are performed. (You may not need to use all the boxes, or you may want to add more.)
- Review your notes—and view the video again, if you wish—to identify cautions or warnings that should be included in the instructions. Decide where these cautions or warnings belong in the instructions, and add them. Use the circles on the flowchart to record them, and indicate their locations with arrows.
- On a separate piece of paper, prepare your instructions for operating the backup Teleprompter. Remember to begin the document with a title and a brief summary of the task. List the needed supplies or equipment, if appropriate. Then list the steps in chronological order. Refer to the section on **Writing Instructions** for help in composing the steps.
- Based on what you have learned from the video and from the directions in this lesson for creating a mechanism description, write a description of the old Teleprompter mechanism.

Continued on page 58

"The most important thing about teleprompting is the speed of the Teleprompter. Can't go too fast—you lose the anchors. Can't go too slow—you lose the audience at home."

Planning Flowchart

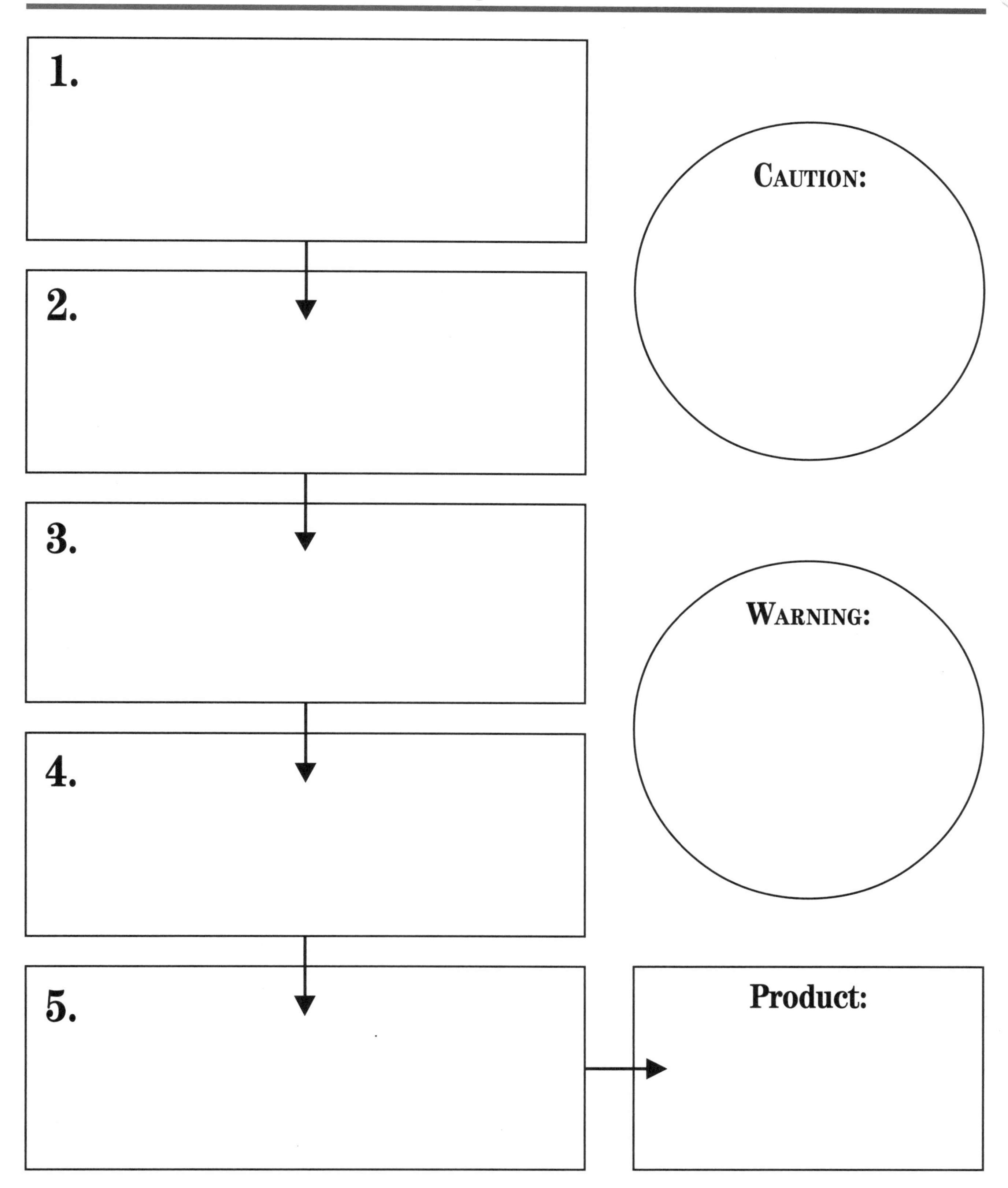

- Decide where this description should be placed, and then insert it in your instructions.
- Decide what diagram or diagrams, if any, should be used, and determine where they should appear in the instructions and/ or the mechanism description.

Be prepared to share your instructions and mechanism description with the class, and keep them in your portfolio.

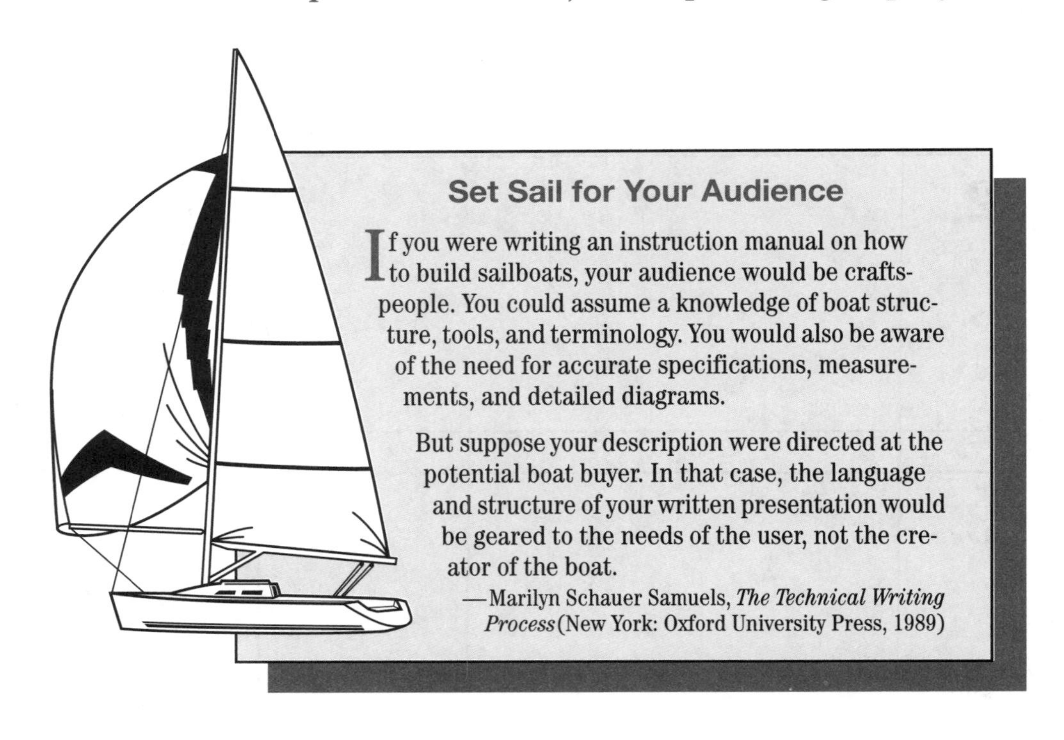

Set Sail for Your Audience

If you were writing an instruction manual on how to build sailboats, your audience would be craftspeople. You could assume a knowledge of boat structure, tools, and terminology. You would also be aware of the need for accurate specifications, measurements, and detailed diagrams.

But suppose your description were directed at the potential boat buyer. In that case, the language and structure of your written presentation would be geared to the needs of the user, not the creator of the boat.

—Marilyn Schauer Samuels, *The Technical Writing Process* (New York: Oxford University Press, 1989)

Summing Up

Pulling It Together

Review the instructions you wrote at the beginning of this lesson. Also review the feedback you received from the student who reviewed your instructions. From what you have learned in this lesson, would you make any changes in the way you organized or wrote the instructions? Would you change the placement of cautions or warnings?

Revise your instructions to reflect any changes. Begin them with a title and brief explanation. If appropriate, near the beginning include a list of necessary materials or tools. Be sure to check that the steps are in chronological order and that only one instruction is included in each step. Put in any cautions or warnings. Check the wording for parallel structure, active voice, and imperative mood.

Be prepared to share your revised instructions with the class. Keep them in your portfolio for future reference.

Keeping Track

On a separate sheet of paper, answer the following questions. Use what you have learned in this lesson to help you.

1 Why is it important to understand both your audience and the task when you are writing instructions?

2 What does it mean to write instructions in the active voice and the imperative mood?

3 What information should a mechanism description contain?

If Carmen had been given better instructions, she would have had less trouble with the Teleprompter.

Going Further

- The British writer Samuel Johnson once wrote that "the second best thing, after being familiar with a subject, is knowing where to find information concerning that subject." If you have access to the Internet, you can find useful information on nearly any subject by subscribing to a newsgroup. Newsgroups are discussion groups of users who are interested in the same topics. Once you subscribe, you can interact with other users by reading, posting, and responding to articles on your topic of interest. Look for a newsgroup that interests you, and follow the instructions for becoming a member and participating in the newsgroup. (Use one of the following newsgroup search engines: Deja News (http://www. dejanews.com/), Liszt (http://www.liszt.com/news/), or Yahoo (http://www.yahoo.com/News/Usenet/). Use what you have learned in this lesson to write a one-page critique of the instructions: How many techniques in this lesson were used, and how

What's in a Name?

The following abbreviations in newsgroup names will help you identify the general subject area of each newsgroup:

alt.	a variety of subject areas
biz.	mainstream business topics
comp.	computer-related
misc.	miscellaneous topics
rec.	recreational
sci.	scientific or medical
soc.	social issues
talk.	discussion, usually of controversial issues

Sample newsgroups include:

comp.archives	Descriptions of public access archives
comp.infosystems.interpedia	The Internet Encyclopedia
misc.news.southasia	News from Bangladesh, India, Nepal, etc.
misc.writing	Discussion of writing in all its forms
rec.crafts.glass	All aspects of glassworking and glass
rec.games.pinball	Discussing pinball-related issues
rec.sport.basketball.women	Women's basketball at all levels
sci.bio.entomology.homoptera	Research on homopteran (sap-sucking) insects
soc.culture.somalia	Somalian affairs, society, and culture
talk.politics.medicine	Politics and ethics of health care

would you improve the instructions? Be prepared to share your critique with the class.

- Think of a task that might be performed by a variety of people. You may choose the task for which you wrote instructions in this lesson or another one—for example, recording or playing a videotape, preparing a simple recipe, or loading a video game on your computer. Then identify three possible users of the instructions you are about to write: someone who is experienced with the equipment or the general process, someone who neither speaks nor reads English, and a young child. Create three sets of instructions for performing the task, adapting each to one type of possible user. Be prepared to turn in your directions to the teacher and to share them with the class.

- Identify someone in your school or community who is responsible for writing instructions. In your school, it might be the office manager who oversees the operation of various pieces of equipment by a number of different people. Or it might be a teacher who regularly writes instructions for examinations. In the community, it might be the person in a factory who is responsible for writing user manuals for machines the company produces. It could be a nurse who writes discharge orders for patients leaving the hospital, or a judge who gives instructions to the jury before they meet to arrive at a verdict. Interview the person to learn how he or she creates instructions; how the instructions may vary, depending upon the audience; and how the instructions are tested for effectiveness. In a one- or two-page paper, compare what the person says with what you have learned in this lesson. Be prepared to turn in your paper to your teacher. With your teacher's permission, you may also wish to invite the person to visit your class and discuss his or her approach to instruction writing.

LESSON 7

Warnings

A Decision-Making Lesson

Looking Ahead

What This Lesson Is About

In this lesson, you will meet a child-care worker who is worried about the increase in infectious diseases among the children in her center. She has an idea for improving the situation, but her supervisor sees no need to do more than the state regulations require.

- Warnings or cautions are an important part of written instructions. They should instruct readers about what they must do, as well as about what they must *not* do.
- Employers are often legally required to provide specific warnings about possible risks associated with the operation of equipment or the use of a product. Failing to do so may result in a lawsuit if customers or employees are injured.
- Employers also have an ethical responsibility to be sure that all warnings and cautions are prominently displayed and clearly stated, so that employees and customers will see them and understand them.

National standards for day-care centers include guidelines on staffing, health protection, facilities, infectious diseases, and children's special needs.

Key Ideas

ethical responsibility—an obligation determined by personal or generally accepted standards of conduct

legal requirement—required by law, with appropriate penalties or punishment for failing to comply

Watch Out!

Take a few minutes to think about the warnings you have come across recently—for example, traffic signs, cautions on over-the-counter allergy medications, warnings about the use or repair of an electrical appliance, or the Surgeon General's warning on a pack of cigarettes. Most likely, each of these warnings satisfied the legal requirements. But were they effective? Did you see them in time to heed the warning? Was the type large enough to read? Did they motivate you to take the recommended precaution—or did you ignore the information?

Choose a warning that you consider to be ineffective. In your journal, identify the warning. Then write a brief set of instructions, directed to the manufacturer, for improving the wording, typographic display, or positioning of the warning to make it more helpful to the user.

Be prepared to share your work with the class.

Getting Started

The Letter vs. the Spirit of the Law

Suppose you are giving a friend directions to your house. "Take Main Street to Willow Road, turn right, go three blocks, and turn left on Fourth Street," you say. "We're the third house from the corner." Ordinarily, those directions might be sufficient, but what if you know that your friend will see Willow *Court* before he reaches Willow Road and might turn there by mistake? To prevent this, you insert a warning: "Pass Willow Court and turn right at the next corner, which is Willow *Road*." By anticipating a problem and steering your reader (or listener) away from it, you provide information on both what to do and what not to do.

The same principle applies to cautions or warnings that appear on many packaged foods, medications, electrical appliances, and other products. A container of whipped topping carries the instruction to "keep refrigerated." However, anticipating that some people may think that, like ice cream, it should go in the freezer, the manufacturer cautions, "Do not freeze." An allergy medication instructs adults to take one tablet every four to six hours, but it warns users to "avoid driving a motor vehicle or operating heavy machinery while taking this product."

Some types of warnings—the Surgeon General's warnings on cigarettes, for example—are required by law, but where and how they are displayed is often left to the judgment of the manufacturer or vendor. The following scenario illustrates the differences between abiding by the letter of the law (acting legally) and carrying out the spirit of the law (acting ethically).

SURGEON GENERAL'S WARNING:
Smoking Causes Lung Cancer, Heart Disease, Emphysema, And May Complicate Pregnancy.

To Shout or to Whisper

When First Planters National Bank decided to charge a flat $20 late fee to credit-card customers who fail to make the minimum payment in any given month, it was required to notify all customers of this change in policy. The advertising department came up with a boxed notification in boldface type that would appear immediately under the "Minimum Payment Due" line on the monthly statement.

"Oh, no, no, no," said the bank's president when he saw the proposed design. "The law says that we must *notify* customers of the charge. It doesn't say that we have to shout it from the rooftops." The banker knew that his firm stood to make a lot of money from these $20 late fees. A customer's minimum payment might be only $5 or $10, but this person would still be required to pay $20 if he missed the payment. "Let's find a way to satisy the regulation without broadcasting the news," the banker said.

When he saw the revised design, he smiled. The announcement of the change in fee was on the reverse side of the invoice and in small type, and it was printed in light-blue ink. What's more, it was buried in the middle of a listing of other disclaimers and possible penalties. "That's more like it," he said. "It's all legal, and there's no reason why we can't whisper, is there?"

Companies that feel an ethical responsibility to communicate a warning effectively will go beyond the letter of the law to make sure that their cautions are

- **clear to the reader.** The vocabulary, concepts, and visuals should be easy to understand. In some cases, this may mean providing the information in more than one language, simplifying the wording, using visual aids, or increasing the size of the type.
- **emphasized in proportion to their importance.** Larger, more serious risks should be displayed more prominently than smaller, less critical ones. Listing all the cautions at the beginning or end of a document makes them appear to be of equal importance.

Warnings: Stating the Obvious?

Some warnings placed on consumer products may seem unnecessary at first glance. Special safety hazards should be listed, of course, but what about obvious dangers? Do consumers need to be warned that knife blades are sharp or that a candle flame can cause painful burns? Does a person who buys a can of paint thinner really need to be told that it can be harmful if swallowed?

Perhaps the old saying "Better safe than sorry" applies here. Whether such warnings are legal requirements or are provided because of ethical responsibilities, they do offer one more level of protection against dangerous situations. And what is obvious to most people may not be obvious to others.

Still, you have to wonder about the situation that led to the following caution's being placed on the instruction sheet for a hand-held hair dryer—as reported by The Laffatorium (www.laffnow.com):

Warning:
Do Not Use While Sleeping

- **appropriately placed.** Warnings should be placed where they will be seen and used—on the lid or opening flap of a package, on or above a piece of equipment, or at a point in a set of directions where the caution should be heeded.

Using what you have read, answer the following questions:

1. In "To Shout or to Whisper" what is the bank's legal requirement?
2. What is its ethical responsibility?
3. What is the difference between a legal requirement and an ethical responsibility?
4. Which design would best fulfill the bank's ethical responsibility? Why? Explain your answer on the basis of clarity, emphasis, and placement.
5. Why is it usually a bad idea to list all warnings or cautions together, perhaps at the beginning or end of a document?

Be prepared to share your answers with the class.

> *"Hand washing is the single most important means of preventing the spread of infection."*
>
> —United States Centers for Disease Control

Trying It Out

Crisis at KiddieKare

In the following scenario, Elena is at odds with her supervisor over the posting of instructions in a child-care center. As you read, think about what Elena should do.

Elena's Problem

Elena is an assistant teacher in the KiddieKare child-care center. She loves her job, and in the short time that she has been there, she has come to know the children and their parents quite well. Recently, however, her relationship with the parents has come into conflict with her relationship with her supervisor, the center director. The issue is the increasing rate of illness among the children in the center. Colds, flu, and, more recently, strep infection have spread quickly, and nearly one-third of the children are absent on any given day.

Several parents had expressed concern to Elena that the staff may not be taking adequate precautions to avoid the spread of germs, and they hinted that they may move their children to another center. Elena shared the parents' comments with the center director, Ms. Nesbitt. The director was furious. "We do everything the state regulations require," she said. "The state says we have to include an infection-control policy and instructions for implementing it in our staff manual. We've done that. Just tell the staff to review the manual—it spells out all the precautions: proper hand washing, food handling, and waste disposal. These parents are just upset because they miss work when their kids get sick. It's not our fault, and I'm not about to do anything more than the state requires. The parents would only see that as an admission of guilt."

Elena didn't argue with Ms. Nesbitt, but she did begin to watch the other child-care workers. Nobody was following the hand-washing standards described in the staff manual and shown on this page; in fact, she saw several staff members merely rinse their hands after diapering a child. No one scrubbed for 10 seconds or used a paper towel to turn off the water. Others went directly from the play area to the kitchen, where they began preparing food without washing up. In the midst of a busy day, they weren't thinking about the instructions in the manual.

The instructions really should be where they're used, Elena thought—over the sink or changing table, with reminders on the kitchen and bathroom doors. And because several of the staff members, like Elena, speak Spanish as a first language, the instructions could be posted in Spanish too.

Elena is willing to take on this project—but she is reluctant to suggest it. After all, Ms. Nesbitt has already made her feelings very clear, and she might interpret Elena's suggestion as a criticism. Elena certainly doesn't want to antagonize her supervisor, because her performance review is coming up soon. On the other hand, if something isn't done, more children will become ill and the center may lose enrollment.

What should Elena do? Should she present her suggestion to Ms. Nesbitt or keep quiet about what she has observed and tell the staff to review the manual?

What Should Elena Do?

What should Elena do? Should she present her suggestion to Ms. Nesbitt? Or should she keep quiet about what she has observed and tell the staff to review the manual? On a separate piece of paper, write your answer to this question, and give your reasons for taking this position.

In deciding what Elena should do, you may find it helpful to outline the issues on a piece of paper. First, list the reasons why

How to Wash Your Hands

Step 1 Use warm, running water. Point hands down.

Step 2 Soap up your hands (liquid soap is preferable).

Step 3 Scrub vigorously for at least 10 seconds.

Step 4 Wash the backs of your hands and wrists, between fingers, and under fingernails thoroughly.

Step 5 Rinse well with warm water.

Step 6 Dry your hands with a paper towel.

Step 7 Turn off the water by using a paper towel—not your clean hands.

Step 8 Throw the paper towel into a pedal-controlled trash can.

Step 9 Put lotion on your hands to prevent cuts or cracks.

—Adapted with permission from the Council for Early Childhood Recognition

When to Wash Your Hands

Staff and children shall wash their hands at least at the following times, and whenever hands are contaminated with body fluids.

- Before food preparation, handling, or serving.
- After toileting or changing diapers.
- After assisting a child with toilet use.
- Before handling food.
- Before any food-service activity (including setting the table).
- Before and after eating meals or snacks.
- After handling pets or other animals.

—American Public Health Association and the American Academy of Pediatrics, *National Health and Safety Performance Standards: Guidelines for Out of Home Child Care Programs* (http://nrc.uchsc.edu/national/index.html)

Elena feels that the center should go beyond the state requirements as far as infection control is concerned. Next, list the reasons why Ms. Nesbitt is opposed to doing more than is required. Then list Elena's two options—(a) present her suggestion to Ms. Nesbitt or (b) keep quiet about what she has observed—and answer the following questions for each option:

1. What will be the short-term consequences for Elena? For the children or their parents? For the center?

2. What will be the long-term consequences for Elena? For the children or parents? For the center?

Be prepared to share with the class your answer to what Elena should do and your reasons for choosing it.

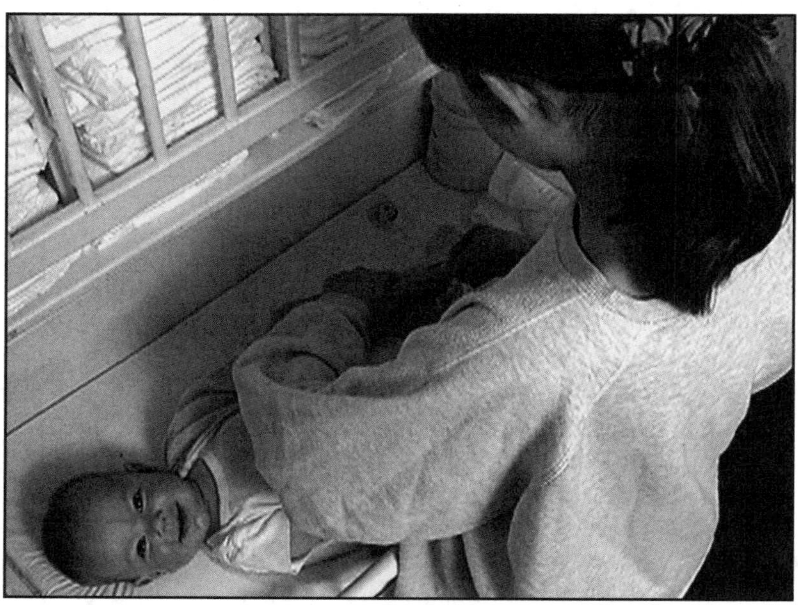

Elena saw a co-worker change a baby's diaper, merely rinse her hands, and then help prepare lunch for the children at the day-care center

Summing Up

Helping Elena Carry Out Her Decision

Based on what you said Elena should do, prepare one of the following documents.

1. If you said that she should communicate her suggestion to the director, draft a memo from Elena to Ms. Nesbitt in which she
    - describes the problem.
    - proposes a solution that will help the staff remember to take the needed infection-control precautions.

- lists the benefits of doing so.
- offers her assistance in implementing the idea.

In writing the memo, you may want to acknowledge Ms. Nesbitt's feelings about the regulations and the parents' complaints and to fit your argument to her concerns.

2 If you said that she should keep quiet to avoid antagonizing Ms. Nesbitt and refer the staff to the manual, draft a memo from Elena to the other staff members. In the memo,

- note that the rate of illness in the center is increasing.
- refer staff to page 13 of the staff manual, where the infection-control policy is explained.
- suggest they review the steps for hand washing, the most important way of curbing the spread of germs.

Be prepared to share your memo with the class.

Room for Improvement

According to a 1997 report of a study by the National Center for the Early Childhood Work Force, only 15 percent of all center-based day care for preschoolers was rated good or excellent, 70 percent was rated mediocre, and 15 percent was considered harmful.

Keeping Track

On a separate sheet of paper, answer the following questions. Use what you have learned in this lesson to help you.

1 What two kinds of instructions do warnings contain?

2 What are the possible legal consequences of failing to provide adequate warnings about risks associated with products or equipment?

3 How does a company's ethical responsibility differ from its legal responsibility in providing warnings or cautions?

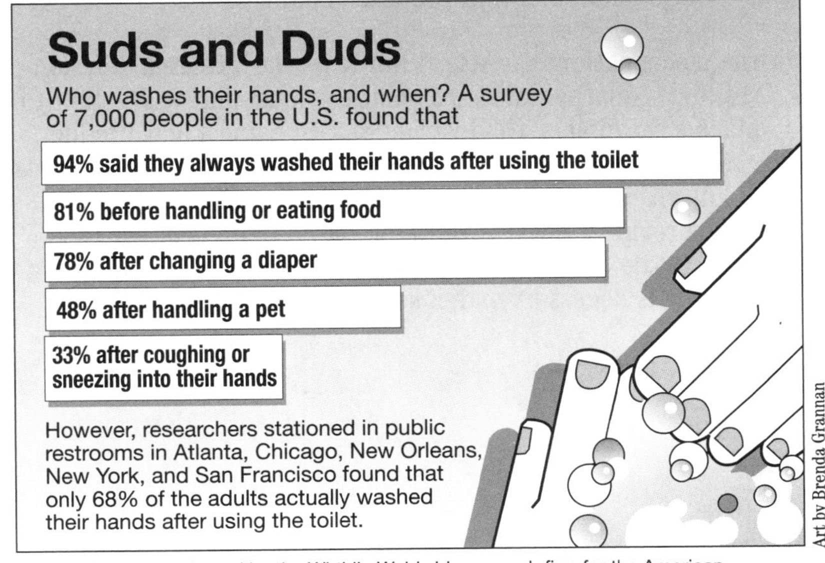

Source: Survey conducted by the Wirthlin Woldwide research firm for the American Society for Microbiology

Going Further

- What role do government agencies play in warning you of possible dangers? Requiring warning labels on products is just one way that government agencies seek to protect the public. In the library or on the Internet, explore a number of government agencies and determine what kinds of warnings each agency might issue. Choose one agency, and write a one-page report describing its responsibilities. Provide two or three examples of warnings the agency has issued. You might want to start your search with a general listing of government agencies, such as the one provided by the Federal Web Locator (http://www.law.vill.edu/fed-agency/fedwebloc.html). Or you may want to explore several of the following agencies: the Occupational Safety and Health Administration (http://www.osha.gov/), the Environmental Protection Agency (http://www.epa.gov), the National Oceanic and Atmospheric Administration (http://www.noaa.gov/), the Food and Drug Administration (http://www.fda.gov), and the U.S. Department of State (http://www.state.gov/). Be prepared to share your report with the class.

- Over the course of several days, collect as many examples of warnings as you can. Look for signs on buses and in public places; read the labels on household cleaning products; check the boxes or package inserts for over-the-counter medicines or creams; look through the manuals for your computer, VCR, or household appliances. Evaluate each by the criteria you studied in this lesson (clarity, emphasis, and appropriate placement). For those that fail the test on at least one criterion, propose a change in design, language, or placement that would make it more useful to the reader. Be prepared to turn in to your teacher a copy of the original warning, your evaluation of it, and your proposed changes.

- In an occupational area that interests you, create a decision-making scenario in which a company must decide whether to place a warning on the instructions for using a new product. Assume that no warning is required by law—but, on the basis of known safety hazards, there may be an ethical responsibility to provide the warning. Be prepared to present your scenario to the class and to lead the discussion about whether a warning is necessary and, if so, how it should be provided.

LESSON 8

Designing Information

A Concept Lesson

Looking Ahead

What This Lesson Is About

In this lesson, you will learn that the appearance of a document plays a major role in communicating its message and in persuading the reader to use the information it contains. Design in technical documents is not merely decoration; each element should add to the persuasiveness and the clarity of the document.

- Information design involves the balancing of three types of elements: textual, spatial, and graphic.
- Strategies such as grouping related items together into chunks, labeling the chunks, and separating them with white space make a document easier to read and understand.
- Graphic devices, color, and shading can add coherence and place emphasis where it belongs.

Key Ideas

bullets—small typographic symbols (usually dots, diamonds, or squares) used to set off items in a list

chunking—grouping related ideas together

font—a specific typeface, distinguished by the style of the letters, numbers, and other characters; traditional printers use the word "font" to refer to a specific size of the typeface (for example, 12-point Helvetica), but today the terms "font" and "typeface" are often used interchangeably

labeling—using headings or subheadings to identify sections of a document or topics within a section

white space—areas in a document (margins, space between columns, or portions of the page) that contain no graphics or type

The ideas and activities in this lesson are adapted from Helen Rothschild Ewald and Rebecca E. Burnett, *Business Communication* (Upper Saddle River, NJ: Prentice-Hall, 1997), 342–365.

Try Your Hand at "Interior Design"

The following information was adapted from the product description and instructions on the package of an over-the-counter cold and allergy medication.

NO-BLO COLD & ALLERGY REMEDY

Each tablet contains two ingredients for the relief of cold and allergy symptoms: an antihistamine (triprolidine) for running nose and sneezing, watery eyes, and itching of the nose or throat and a decongestant (pseudoephedrine) for nasal congestion and stuffiness and swollen sinus passages. Ingredients: pseudoephedrine hydrochloride 60 mg and triprolidine hydrochloride 2.5 mg; flavor, hydroxypropyl methylcellulose, lactose, magnesium stearate, polyethylene glycol, potato starch, povidone, sucrose, and titanium dioxide.

Directions: Adults and children, 12 years of age and over, 1 tablet every 4 to 6 hours. Children 6 to 12 years of age, 1/2 tablet every 4 to 6 hours. Children under 6, consult a physician. No more than 4 doses in 24 hours. May cause excitability in children. May cause drowsiness; in higher doses, may cause nervousness, dizziness, or sleeplessness. If symptoms do not improve within 7 days, consult a physician before continuing use. Do not take this product if you have high blood pressure, heart disease, diabetes, thyroid disease, asthma, glaucoma, or if you are pregnant or nursing a baby. Do not take this product if you are taking a prescription antihypertensive or antidepressant drug containing a monoamine oxidase inhibitor, except under the advice of a physician. Avoid driving a motor vehicle, operating heavy machinery, or drinking alcoholic beverages while taking this product.

Store at 15° to 25°C (59° to 77°F) in a dry, dark place. Keep out of reach of children. In case of accidental overdose, seek professional help or call a Poison Control Center immediately.

Basing your response on what you have learned about instructions and your instincts as a consumer, do you think this information is communicated clearly and persuasively to the reader? If not, how could it be improved?

On a separate piece of paper, list the weaknesses of the instructions and the changes you would make to improve clarity and effectiveness. Save these ideas for use later in this lesson.

Be prepared to share with the class your assessment of the NO-BLO information and your suggestions for improving it.

Getting Started

Appearance Counts

Some writers believe that only words are needed to communicate a message. In many instances, however—particularly in technical writing—the way words are arranged on the page and how they are supported by graphic elements may determine whether the document is understood. Those two factors may even determine whether the message is read at all! Information design involves managing three kinds of elements:

- **Textual**—These elements include the letters, numbers, and symbols that form the words and sentences in your document, as well as headings, labels, and page numbers.
- **Graphic**—These elements include photographs, drawings, diagrams, graphs, and other graphic devices, such as boxes, bullets, and icons.
- **Spatial**—These elements include the placement of blocks of type (textual elements) and graphic devices, such as the use of white space between these items and in the margins of the pages.

Information design should result in a document that is attractive to the eye, but the primary purpose of the design is not decorative. Good information design enhances the persuasive appeal of the document, clarifies its meaning, and establishes the relative importance of the various sections or parts within the document.

Four basic strategies can help you create a design that is both functional and attractive: **chunking information**, **labeling**, **creating coherence**, and **establishing emphasis**.

1. **Chunking information.** Good writing of any type "chunks" information. It's called organization, and it means grouping related ideas and thoughts together. Information design takes the process one step further by ensuring that the chunks are visually separated—by white space, headings, or graphic devices. This helps the reader to see at a glance the various parts of a document and how they relate to one another.
2. **Labeling.** By labeling the chunks of information with headings and subheadings, you provide "road signs" to help your reader locate the various sections of the document and the topics covered within each section. The size and style of type that you use for headings, as well as the use of different levels of indentation, can establish the relative importance of the various parts.
3. **Creating coherence.** It is important to provide a consistent "look" for any document. This can be achieved by using the same font (or fonts) and basic layout throughout the document. You might decide, for example, to use a two- or three-column format. You may choose one font for the text and another for the headings, or you may use bullets, symbols, or icons to identify major headings and subheadings. All of these designs should be maintained throughout the document to provide visual consistency and coherence. Similarly, any use

The Wisdom of White Space

One key to using white space effectively is to understand that the reader's eye is intuitively attracted to white, so elements with a lot of space around them get more attention. The reader perceives elements spaced closely together as being connected and those spaced apart as separate. Thus, the correct use of white space is vital to any printed piece.

—Philip Brady, *Using Type Right* (Cincinnati: North Light Books, 1988) of color or shaded areas should also be consistent throughout the document.

4. **Establishing emphasis.** In most technical documents, some sections need special emphasis to ensure that they are not overlooked. These sections may be safety warnings, cautions about the use of the equipment, or simply important steps or facts that should be "flagged" for the reader. Color and/or the use of boldface type are probably the most effective ways to highlight particular words or sections. Other devices for emphasis include icons, graphic figures such as arrows or lines, and variations in type style or size. (Typography is further considered in Lesson 9.)

In designing a technical document, it is important to remember that more is not necessarily better. Too much color or too many different colors, for example, can diminish effectiveness in providing emphasis. Too much detail in a graph, called "chartjunk," can make it less dramatic. And too much creativity—such as printing text over a photograph or using a light- or bright-colored ink for a large block of type—may be effective from an artistic point of view, but by reducing the readability of the document, these techniques defeat the purpose of information design.

In considering any strategy, ask yourself,

> "Will this element encourage people to read it? Will it help the reader understand what I am saying?"

If the answer to either question is no, go back to the drawing board.

Using what you have read, answer the following questions:

1 What is "chunking," and why is it an important design strategy?

2 What purposes are served by headings and subheadings (labeling) in technical documents?

3 What strategies can provide coherence and emphasis to a document?

Be prepared to share your answers with the class.

Projecting the Corporate Image

If you know how to control the visual elements of the page, the page will look professional, creating a positive impression of your document, the product, and your company. That is why large companies develop corporate design formats for their books. Companies such as Xerox Corporation and Apple Computer go to great lengths to make their documents visually consistent. They're not trying to be dictatorial; they're trying to create a polished, corporate "look" that readers will recognize and trust.

—Adapted from Janet Van Wicklen, *The Tech Writing Game* (New York: Facts on File, 1992)

Here's How It's Done

In the following scenario, a veterinary technician redesigns an instruction sheet for pet owners. Look for the ways she uses the four design strategies and how they improve the document.

Postoperative Care for Dogs and Cats

"Our rate of complications after surgery is way too high," Dr. Growley complained one day to his staff. "It's not our fault. The pet owners aren't reading the instructions we give them—or, at any rate, they're not following them."

> ***"Regardless of the devices that are conjured up by the technicians, designers have the last word with the words."***
>
> —*Upper & Lower Case* magazine

Jennifer, a veterinary technician who has taken courses in communication, suggested gently that the instructions could be better organized and more attractive. Holding up a copy of the handout that owners receive after their pets have surgery, she went on: "Everything is right here, but it's hard to see at a glance what you should do."

Dr. Growley, who had written the instructions himself, was skeptical. But he wanted to reduce the rate of complications before the clinic started losing customers. "Fine," he said to Jennifer. "Redesign it, and we'll all take a look at it before it's printed."

Here's the original instruction sheet:

> Instructions
>
> Now that your pet's surgery is over, it is up to you to help it recover fully. For the next 10 days to two weeks, you will need to monitor its activity, diet, and incision to avoid any complications.
>
> Treat your pet's recent surgery as you would your own. Limit activity and be sure the pet gets plenty of rest and relaxation. Fresh air and moderate exercise are important, but for the first week, keep your pet quiet and restrict activity. Discourage running and jumping. Block off staircases, and consider keeping the pet in a cage at night. Keep your pet on a leash during outdoor exercise, to avoid contact with other animals. Moderation is the key to maintaining your pet's diet after surgery. Anesthesia may cause an upset stomach, so withhold all food and drink for the first 12 hours after surgery. For the next several days, reduce the food to one-third to one-half of the usual amount. Allow only small amounts of water at a time. If the doctor has prescribed a special diet, follow directions carefully. Protect the incision site. Your pet has several layers of sutures (stitches). Check the incision site every day until your pet returns to have the sutures removed (usually 10 days to two weeks after surgery). If you see any swelling, discharge, or drainage, or if the sutures stretch, tear, or are removed, call the clinic immediately.

Jennifer's first step was to chunk the information by dividing the instructions into four sections: an introduction, followed by instructions for limiting activity, providing a healthy diet, and protecting the incision. Under each topic, she listed the separate instructions. Then she labeled the sections by inserting headings and subheadings.

Here's how the instructions looked after she completed these preliminary design steps:

> Caring for Your Pet after Surgery
>
> Now that your pet's surgery is over, it is up to you to help it recover fully. For the next 10 days to two weeks, you will need to monitor its activity, diet, and incision to avoid any complications.
>
> Monitor Pet's Activity
>
> Treat your pet's surgery as you would your own.
>
> Limit activity and be sure the pet gets plenty of rest and relaxation. Fresh air and moderate exercise are important, but for the first week, keep your pet quiet and restrict activity.
>
> Discourage running and jumping. Block off staircases, and consider keeping the pet in a cage at night.
>
> Keep your pet on a leash during outdoor exercise, to avoid contact with other animals.
>
> Maintain a Healthy Diet
>
> Moderation is the key to maintaining your pet's diet after surgery.
>
> Anesthesia may cause an upset stomach, so withhold all food and drink for the first 12 hours after surgery.
>
> For the next several days, reduce the food to one-third to one-half of the usual amount.
>
> Allow only small amounts of water at a time. If the doctor has prescribed a special diet, follow directions carefully.
>
> Protect the Incision Site
>
> Your pet has several layers of sutures (stitches).
>
> Check the incision site every day until your pet returns to have the sutures removed (usually 10 days to two weeks after surgery).
>
> If you see any swelling, discharge, or drainage, or if the sutures stretch, tear, or are removed, call the clinic immediately.

Jennifer showed her revision to Barbara, the receptionist who deals regularly with clients. "That's a big improvement," Barbara said, "but can we make the headings stand out more, emphasize the most important points, and use something to tie the whole piece together?" Back at her computer, Jennifer considered the issue of emphasis. She decided to use bullets to set the points off—one kind of bullet for the main headings, another for the subheadings. She put the title in larger type and used dark backgrounds to set off the three main points. Finally, she put the key words in boldface type. If Dr. Growley decided to print the flyer in color, she reasoned, the backgrounds and boldface

"Always design a thing by considering it in its next larger context—a chair in a room, a room in a house, a house in an environment, an environment in a city plan."

—Eliel Saarinen, American (Finnish-born) architect

words could be in color. Then she checked to make sure that various sizes of headings, fonts, bullets, and boldface type were used consistently throughout the document.

When Jennifer passed out copies of her revised instruction sheet, the staff applauded her. Even Dr. Growley was pleased. "You've really worked a miracle," he said.

Be prepared to discuss this scenario in class and to compare Jennifer's strategies with the design tips you learned in **Appearance Counts.**

Caring for Your Pet after Surgery

Now that your pet's surgery is over, it is up to you to help it recover fully. For the next 10 days to two weeks, you will need to monitor its activity, diet, and incision to avoid any complications.

Monitor Pet's Activity

▶ Treat your pet's surgery as you would your own.

- Limit activity and be sure the pet gets plenty of rest and relaxation. Fresh air and moderate exercise are important, but for the first week, keep your pet quiet and restrict activity.
- Discourage running and jumping. Block off staircases, and consider keeping the pet in a cage at night.
- Keep your pet on a leash during outdoor exercise, to avoid contact with other animals.

Maintain a Healthy Diet

▶ Moderation is the key to maintaining your pet's diet after surgery.

- Anesthesia may cause an upset stomach, so withhold all food and drink for the first 12 hours after surgery.
- For the next several days, reduce the food to one-third to one-half of the usual amount.
- Allow only small amounts of water at a time. If the doctor has prescribed a special diet, follow directions carefully.

Protect the Incision Site

▶ The incision must be kept clean to avoid infection.

- Your pet has several layers of sutures (stitches). Check the incision site every day until your pet returns to have the sutures removed (usually 10 days to two weeks after surgery).
- If you see any swelling, discharge, or drainage, or if the sutures stretch, tear, or are removed, call the clinic immediately: **555-MEOW.**

Raintree Animal Hospital, 231 DogLeg Road, 555-6369

Graphical Elements

Jennifer could also use a photograph or drawing to add visual appeal to her instruction sheet.

Trying It Out

Dissecting Documents

Spend some time examining several documents to see whether they reflect the principles you learned about in this lesson.

1. Locate at least three examples of informational material. You may find some in your classroom or school—a textbook, a computer manual or documentation that you can print out from a "Read Me" file or a CD-ROM, a student handbook, or an announcement on the bulletin board. At home, you may find a brochure from a car dealership, an instruction manual for a VCR, or a prospectus (description) of an insurance plan. Bring the documents, or photocopies of them, to class.
2. Using copies of the **Information Design Assessment** form on page 78, evaluate each of your examples from the standpoint of their textual, spatial, and graphic elements.
3. In any areas that you identify as weak, suggest ways that the document could be improved through use of the design strategies you learned in this lesson.

Be prepared to share your evaluations with the class.

Divide and Conquer

The designer should group elements into short chunks surrounded by white frames of space. If your page looks like the white pages of the telephone directory, the reader will read it only if it is urgent.

—Marvin Jacobs, *Graphic Design for Desktop Dummies*
(Cleveland: Ameritype & Art Inc., 1993)

Summing Up

Back to Square One

Review the NO-BLO package information at the beginning of this lesson. Now that you know more about information design, would you change your original assessment and suggestions? If so, how?

Using questions from the **Information Design Assessment** form, decide whether the various strategies were used appropriately in the NO-BLO directions. Then, imagining that you are a supervisor in the product-information division, draft a memo to the writer who prepared the package description. Your memo should point out the weaknesses of the description and offer concrete suggestions for improving it.

Be prepared to share your memo with the class.

Keeping Track

On a separate sheet of paper, answer the following questions. Use what you have learned in this lesson to help you.

1. What are the three elements that must be balanced in information design?
2. What are four ways of using design principles to make a document easier to read and to understand?
3. What is the primary function of color, shading, and graphic devices in technical documents?

Going Further

- Choose one of the examples you assessed in **Trying It Out** or the NO-BLO description in the opening activity (**Try Your Hand at "Interior Design"**). With your critique of it as your basis, create a new design that incorporates the principles and strategies you learned in this lesson. If possible, use a computer to create your document. Be prepared to turn in your design to your teacher and to share it with the class.
- Spend an hour or two exploring the Internet to find good examples of information design on Web pages. Print out two or three pages that you consider very effective—inviting to the reader and easy to understand. Assess them for chunking, labeling, coherence, and appropriate emphasis, as well as for the effective use of space and color. In a one- or two-page paper, compare information design in print vs. electronic media. Turn in your paper, along with the printout of the pages you examined, to your teacher.
- Identify a graphic designer—either an independent consultant or a staff member of an advertising agency—in your community. Arrange an interview with this person to discuss his or her approach to designing various informational pieces—manuals, packaging, and documents such as proposals and instructions. Compare what you learn with the principles and strategies presented in this lesson. Summarize in your journal any new ideas or strategies that come out of your meeting. With your teacher's permission, invite the designer to visit your school and to share work samples and ideas with the entire class.

Web Design

Look for good examples of design on the World Wide Web in the following sites:

- Best of the Web (http://www.botw.org/)
- The Internet Professional Publishers Association IPPA Award for Design Excellence (http://www.ippa.org/)
- Lycos Top 5% (http://www.pointcom.com/categories/)
- The Médaille d'Or for Web Site Excellence (http://www.arachnid.co.uk/award/award.html)
- The Web 100 (http://www.web100.com/)

Activity Form

Information Design Assessment

Your Name ______________________ Sample Assessed ______________________

Criteria	Yes	No	If "No," Suggested Improvement
TEXTUAL ELEMENTS			
1. Is the information divided by topic into chunks?			
2. Are the major sections of the document labeled with headings and subheadings?			
3. Is the wording clear and concise?			
SPATIAL ELEMENTS			
4. Is white space used effectively to make the document appear uncrowded and inviting?			
5. Are the lines of text adequately spaced to promote readability?			
GRAPHIC ELEMENTS			
6. Is color used effectively to provide coherence and emphasis?			
7. Are graphic devices used consistently and effectively?			
Does the overall design make the user want to read it? Do the design elements help to communicate the message?			

LESSON 9

Creating a Design

A Concept Lesson

Looking Ahead

What This Lesson Is About

In this lesson, you will learn more about using various typefaces and other layout and typographical devices to make users more likely to read and understand the information you want to share with them. To give you a chance to apply what you learn, you will also design a set of instructions.

- Technical documents should be attractive to the reader, but the top priority is to make the document easier to read and to understand.
- Research has shown that some typestyles (for example, all capital letters, sans serif fonts, and italics) make text more difficult to read. They should be used sparingly.
- Formatting is also an important factor for readability.

An effective design uses typestyle and formatting to make the document easier to read.

Key Ideas

highlighters—variations in a typeface, used to draw attention to specific words or phrases

justification—the process of spacing out lines of type so that the ends of the lines are even

point—a unit of measurement for type (one point is approximately 1/72 of an inch)

sans serif type—typeface (font) without the decorative "tails" (serifs)

serif type—typeface (font) with tiny fine lines (or "tails"), usually on the tops or bottoms of letters

tombstoning—an unintentional alignment of headings in two adjoining columns

widow—an incomplete line of type that falls at the top or bottom of a column

Which Do You Prefer?

Here are two versions of the same instructions for giving first aid to victims of serious burns. Which would you be most likely to read? Which instructions would you be most likely to remember in an emergency situation?

Version A

Cool a burn by flushing with water. **DON'T APPLY ICE DIRECTLY TO ANY BURN.** Cover the burn with a dry, cool covering, such as a sterile dressing. **DON'T TOUCH A BURN WITH ANYTHING THAT IS NOT CLEAN. DON'T REMOVE PIECES OF CLOTH THAT STICK TO THE BURNED AREA. DON'T BREAK BLISTERS. DON'T USE OINTMENT ON A SEVERE BURN.** Keep the victim comfortable. Avoid chilling or overheating.

Version B

DOs:

- **Cool** a burn by flushing with water.
- **Cover** the burn with a dry, cool covering, such as a sterile dressing.
- Keep the victim **comfortable**; avoid chilling or overheating.

DON'Ts

- Do **NOT** apply ice directly to any burn.
- Do **NOT** touch a burn with anything that is not clean.
- Do **NOT** remove pieces of cloth that stick to the burned area
- Do **NOT** break blisters.
- Do **NOT** use ointment on a severe burn.

—Adapted from *American Red Cross Community First Aid & Safety* (St. Louis: Mosby Lifeline, 1993)

Help with Headings

- Choose a type font, style, size, and position for each heading and subheading.
- Treat headings as though they were illustrations to the text—they must be relevant to the text content in both style and theme.

—Adapted from David Collier and Bob Cotton, *Basic Desktop Design and Layout* (Cincinnati: North Light Books, 1989)

When you have selected the version that you think is most appealing and readable, compare the one you selected with the less readable version. What are the factors that led you to choose one over the other? On a separate piece of paper, explain why you would be more likely to read and to remember the instructions in the version you chose.

Be prepared to discuss your choice and your list of factors with the class. Keep your paper for use later in this lesson.

Getting Started

The Finer Points of Design

Lesson 8 focused on basic principles of information design, including organizing your material into chunks and labeling the chunks with headings and subheadings. It also considered the need to create coherence by using typefaces and spacing consistently throughout the document. Finally, it showed how graphic devices (such as boxes), color, and type highlighters (such as boldface, capital letters, and italics) can be used to emphasize key words or paragraphs.

In this lesson, you will learn more about using typography, graphics, and page layout to make your document easier to read and understand, as well as more attractive.

Types of Type

If you are an experienced computer user, you know that typefaces come in many different families—families with such names as Times New Roman, Garamond, Helvetica, New Baskerville, and Letter Gothic. Within each family (called a "font"), you may choose from a wide range of sizes (measured in "points") and several different forms, such as **boldface**, *italic*, shadow, outline, and SMALL CAPS. These forms are called highlighters, because they are used to call attention to specific words or phrases by changing the appearance of the letters. There are also a number of specialty fonts, such as Shelly Allegro.

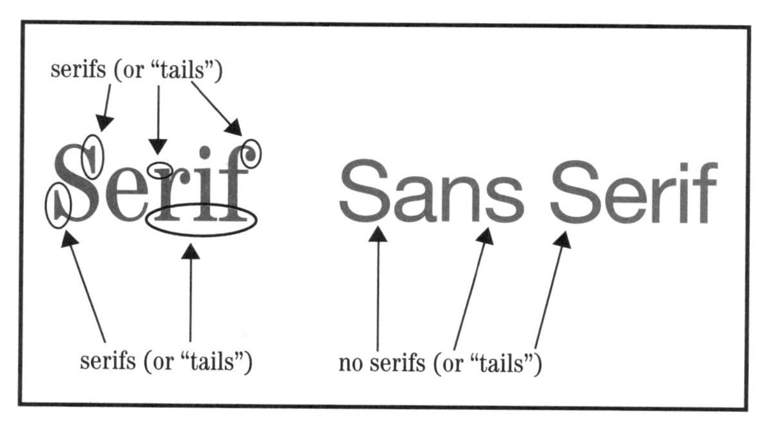

Most type fonts can be categorized as either "serif" or "sans serif." Serif type, like that used in this book, is designed with tiny fine lines at the beginning and end of the strokes that form the letters. The Times New Roman, Garamond, and New Baskerville fonts mentioned earlier are examples of serif typefaces. Sans serif faces, like those used for the subheadings in this book, have clean lines with no decoration or "tails." Helvetica and Letter Gothic are examples of sans serif typefaces.

Using Boldface and Italics for Emphasis

Use **bold** and *italic* forms of your text typeface when you want to emphasize certain words.

Using bold type is effective, but it has a drawback: boldface type is somewhat harder to read than roman type. Italic emphasis is more subtle and doesn't affect readability.

You can use bold and italics to establish a two-tier system so that different types of emphasis are used consistently. But remember, overuse of emphasis is irritating and counterproductive.

—Adapted from David Collier and Bob Cotton, *Basic Desktop Design and Layout* (Cincinnati: North Light Books, 1989)

Research has been conducted on how people react to variations in typography. This research reveals the following:

- Most people find it easier to read serif fonts than sans serif ones, particularly in long documents. Sans serif faces, however, can be used effectively for headings and in short documents.
- The least readable—and least likely to be read—is text that is set entirely in capital letters (all caps). Using larger type, boldface, or a combination of caps and small caps is much more effective for calling attention to specific elements in a document.
- Italics and specialty fonts (for example, Shelly Allegro) are appropriate for certain documents, such as invitations, or for small sections of larger documents. In longer bodies of text, however, they are more difficult to read than regular (or "roman") type.

Choose a Font, Paint a Picture

Fonts are like abstract pictures; each one carries a message of style. Make sure that the font you choose is relevant to the style of the text content. Serif fonts are generally more traditional in feel; sans serif fonts are more modern. Typewriter fonts are more folksy, script fonts very romantic, bold fonts very forceful.

—Adapted from David Collier and Bob Cotton, *Basic Desktop Design and Layout* (Cincinnati: North Light Books, 1989)

Just as combining too many patterns or colors in clothing or using too much makeup can defeat the goal of looking attractive, overusing highlighters or specialty fonts can confuse and annoy readers. For most documents, two fonts are enough—one for the text and one for headings. Use highlighters only for those words or phrases that require strong emphasis, such as cautions and warnings.

Based on what you have read, answer the following questions:

1. What is the difference between serif and sans serif typefaces?
2. What kind of typeface is believed to be easier to read?
3. For what purpose are highlighters used?

Be prepared to share your answers with the class.

Format

The formatting of a document includes several factors:

Column grids. The layout, or grid, you use for your document will depend in part on the purpose of the document and the overall size of the finished product. As a general rule, letters, memos, and reports, including proposals, use a single-column format, filling the area between the page margins (see Figure 1 on the next page). In some cases, however, these documents use a two-column grid, with headings and/or graphics placed in one column (Figure 2). Manuals and brochures typically use a two-column format (Figure 3), and newsletters often use a three-column format (Figure 4). In general, a shorter line length (three to four inches) is easier to read than a wider one.

Justification. Within a column, the lines of type are usually lined up so that they are even along the left margin (called "left

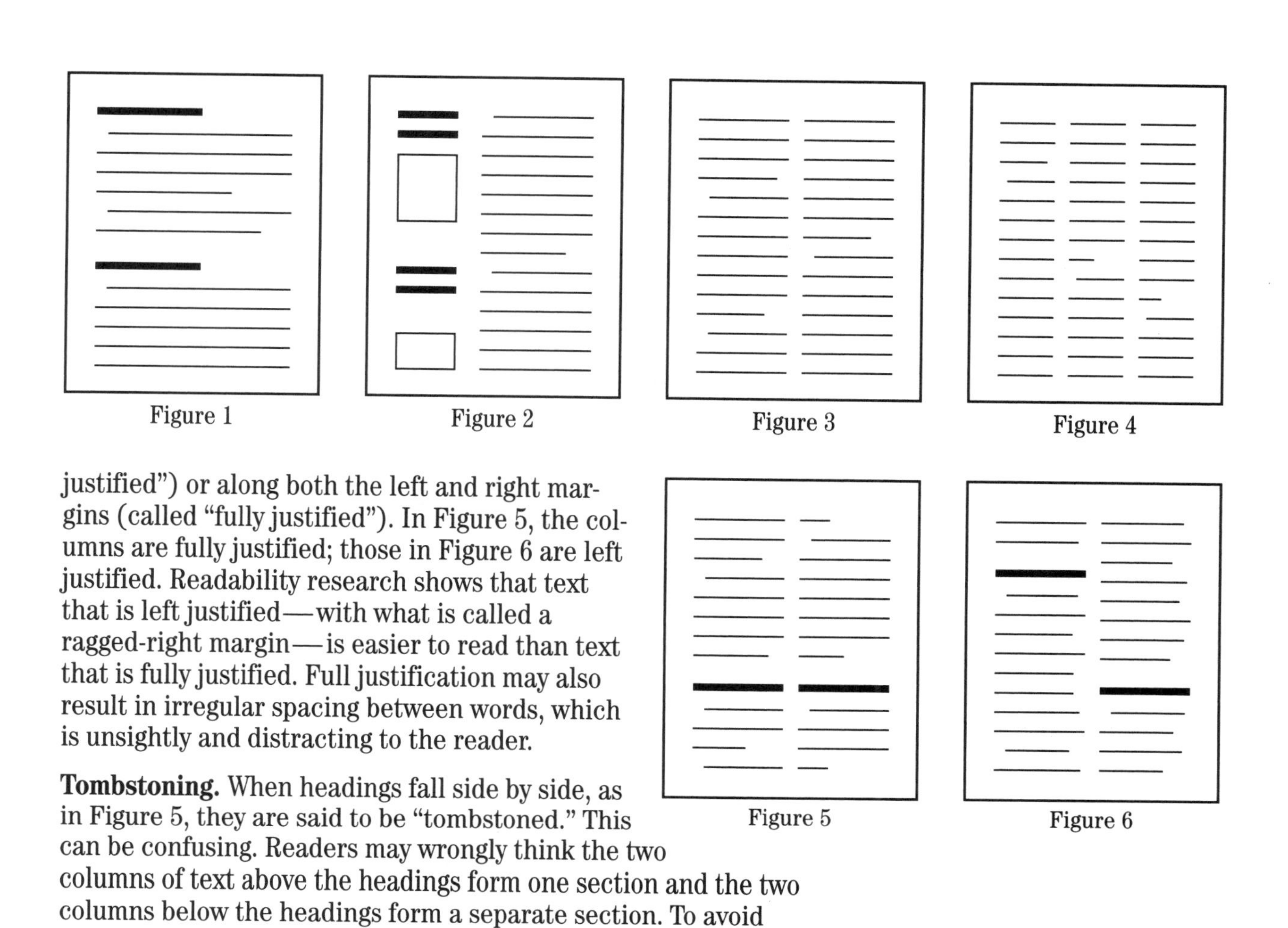

Figure 1 Figure 2 Figure 3 Figure 4

Figure 5 Figure 6

justified") or along both the left and right margins (called "fully justified"). In Figure 5, the columns are fully justified; those in Figure 6 are left justified. Readability research shows that text that is left justified—with what is called a ragged-right margin—is easier to read than text that is fully justified. Full justification may also result in irregular spacing between words, which is unsightly and distracting to the reader.

Tombstoning. When headings fall side by side, as in Figure 5, they are said to be "tombstoned." This can be confusing. Readers may wrongly think the two columns of text above the headings form one section and the two columns below the headings form a separate section. To avoid this, the text or headings should be rearranged, or an illustration or white space can be inserted.

Widows. Another formatting problem occurs when a single line, usually short, winds up at the top or bottom of a column, as in Figure 5, right column. This results in "widows," and the harm they do is largely in appearance. Avoid them by editing the text. (Note: A widow also occurs when the first line of a new paragraph is at the bottom of a column, as in Figure 5, left column.)

Leading. The space between lines is called "leading" (pronounced "ledding"). When text blocks are long and not broken up by bulleted items or subheadings or when the type is small (eight points or less), single spacing is often hard to read. If a page of type looks too dense to read comfortably, add more space between the lines. (Consult your software user's manual to see how to add leading.)

Based on what you have read, respond to the following:

1 Name three common formats or grids for technical documents.

2 Name two disadvantages of full justification of lines of type.

3 What is tombstoning, and why should it be avoided?

Be prepared to share your answers with the class.

Trying It Out

Design Your Instructions

Lesson 6 asked you to create a set of instructions for operating the Teleprompter and a description of how that device works. Those two documents can serve as an attachment to a proposal in Lesson 12, where you are asked to write a proposal to the management of Channel 3, urging them to improve the training of employees. The mechanism description and the instructions for operating a Teleprompter are examples of the kinds of materials that the TV station should provide to its employees; therefore, it is important for these documents to look professional and to be both inviting to read and easy to understand.

Use word-processing or desktop-publishing software to design your instructions and mechanism description. Lessons 8 and 9 offer many valuable tips for designing professional documents. To create your design, use this checklist:

☑ Choose the size and format of the document. Because it will be attached to an 8½-inch by 11-inch proposal and may eventually be part of a manual for interns, you may want to begin with an 8½-inch by 11-inch page. Then,

☑ Review your instructions in light of what you have learned about design, and make sure that

- the information is logically organized and divided into appropriate "chunks."
- the chunks are labeled with headings and subheadings.
- you have identified the words, phrases, or instructions that should be emphasized.
- your use of design elements is consistent.

☑ Plan your design.

- Decide what grid you will use (one, two, or three columns) and whether you will use left or full justification. Determine whether an adjustment in leading is desirable.
- Choose a font (or fonts) and type size (or sizes) for the document and for the headings.

  (The grid and typefaces can be set up as automatic functions within your computer's word-processing or desktop-publishing program.)
- Decide which form or typographical device you will use for the highlighted items.
- Choose any illustrations or graphics you plan to use.

☑ Design your instructions on the computer.

Design Tips

- Place more white space above a heading than below it.
- Slightly increase the space between lines as you increase the length of the text line. This will maintain readability.
- Develop an "ideas file" of eye-catching designs. Look for examples in newspapers, magazines, advertising, brochures, books.

—Philip Brady, *Using Type Right* (Cincinnati: North Light Books, 1988)

☑ Run the spell-check, and print a draft copy. Review it critically, looking for widows, tombstones, and any other problems that may have occurred in the formatting. Check your document for consistency of design. Carefully proofread the document to catch any typographical errors that the spell-check missed. Correct the errors you found on your computer file, save it to disk, and print out another copy.

Save your work, and keep a hard copy in your portfolio.

Choosing Your Column Width

Is this column too wide for comfortable reading? In *Design Principles for Desktop Publishers* (Belmont, CA: Wadsworth, 1994), Tom Lichty recommends a maximum column width of about 2.5 lowercase alphabets of the font and size in use. He suggests 1.5 alphabets as the minimum. (The column you are now reading is about three alphabets wide.)

Summing Up

Burn Care Revisited

Review the critique of the burn-care instructions that you wrote at the beginning of this lesson. Look again at the two versions of the instructions. Would you still choose the same one as the more effective design? Now look at your list of the factors that made one version better than the other.

On the basis of what you have learned in this lesson, would you add anything to your list? What suggestions would you have for improving even the better version? Write your response to these questions on a separate piece of paper.

Be prepared to discuss your comments and suggestions with the class.

Keeping Track

On a separate sheet of paper, respond to the following items. Use what you have learned in this lesson to help you.

1. In choosing a grid or a font, what should be your first priority?
2. Why should highlighters and special fonts be used sparingly?
3. List three factors in formatting that help the reader understand a document.

Going Further

- Call the community-relations director or public-service director of a television station in your city. Describe the project you are working on in this course, and ask permission to visit the station and see the Teleprompter in action. If possible, arrange to interview the staff member who programs the information into the Teleprompter and the one who operates it during a newscast. Compare what you learn with the information you gathered from the videos, and summarize the similarities and differences in a brief paper. Be prepared to turn in your work to your teacher. Be prepared to discuss your visit with the class.

- If you completed the **Information Design Assessment** form in Lesson 8, reexamine the materials you evaluated. This time look closely at the choice of typeface, the spacing, the layout grid, and the use of highlighters. Check for problems, such as tombstoning and widows. Write an addendum to your original evaluation by assessing the material from the standpoint of these design elements. Be prepared to turn in your paper to your teacher.

- The design of fonts or type families has been a proud tradition in the printing industry for hundreds of years. Many fonts bear the name of their designer (for example, Bodoni, Garamond, Goudy, and Cheltenham). In your library, research the background of one or more fonts, learning all you can about the designer and the reason a particular font was designed. On the internet, you may want to look at Type-Related Organizations (http://desktoppublishing.com/fonts-org.html) and TypeRight Links (http://www.typeright.org/links.html). Summarize what you learn in a one- or two-page paper. Be prepared to turn in your paper to your teacher and to share it with the class.

LESSON 10

Testing and Revising

A Strategies Lesson

Looking Ahead

What This Lesson Is About

In this lesson, you will test and revise instructions.

- Writers assess the accuracy and appeal of their written instructions and other documents by any of the following three methods: text-based, expert-based, and user-based testing.
- To carry out this testing, writers seek content, structural, editorial, and design feedback from readers of their draft documents.
- Using the feedback they receive, writers revise their documents to make them as accurate and appealing as possible.

Key Ideas

draft—the preliminary form of a document that will be revised

feedback—information obtained from reader response to a document

revision—the corrected and improved form of a draft document

A Document Revisited

Lesson 6 gave you the opportunity to create instructions and a mechanism description to show people how to operate a Teleprompter. In Lesson 9, you used design techniques to make a document more readable, attractive, and useful.

Take a fresh look at the hard copy of the document you designed. View it objectively. Try to look at it through the eyes of other people who may read, critique, or use your document.

On a separate sheet of paper, make a list of any elements of your document that could be improved. Do not limit your critique to design elements—look for misplacement of major points, unclear wording, and misspellings. For example, if you notice that an important point is unclear, out of place, or missing, make a note of it. If you see a word that is misspelled or misused, write it down. (Don't count on a spell-check program to catch all your spelling and usage mistakes. Spell-checkers won't catch such errors as the use of "their" instead of "there.") If you think of a design technique that might improve your draft, note that too. And if you see nothing at all wrong with your draft, write a statement to that effect.

Keep your list handy for use later in this lesson.

Getting Started

The Need to Revise

When people complete the first draft of a document, they often think that they are finished—that the document is as good as it can be. But that is only a first draft. No workplace document is complete until it is tested and revised. That may mean changing a single misspelled word, reordering paragraphs, or completely rewriting a document. Remember that an effective document is one that works for the audience and attains its purpose.

If you take pride in your writing or designing abilities, you may shudder at the thought of changing what you've created. Taking pride in your work is good—most successful writers do. But don't let your pride keep you from looking objectively at your work or from accepting constructive feedback from people who read it.

Always remember that in workplace writing the most important thing is not your own feelings but the creation of a document that will be of use to someone else. To achieve greater accuracy and appeal, you may need to revise any document that you produce.

Be prepared to discuss with your classmates the need for revising a document.

Light Speed or No Speed?

Revising your document is especially important when it involves detailed technical information. If there are errors in such a document, your readers could have serious problems.

One editor reports that a freelance writer sent her an article on "Bringing Your Windows to Light Speed," and she then tested the document with an expert—a software programmer. They ran through the writer's tips and tricks and found nothing wrong, but when the article was published, all was not well. It seemed the writer had neglected to mention in his article that his tips were applicable only for computers running a certain version of Windows in conjunction with a certain limited version of DOS. As a result, the editor received hundreds of calls from readers with computers whose Windows weren't at light speed—they were crashed.

With the help of a couple of textbooks and some knowledgeable staff members, the editor solved the problem, but it was a lesson she won't forget.

—Adapted from Angela D. Mitchell, "10 Hot Tips for Writing High Tech," *Writer's Digest* (March 1997)

Testing

The revision process consists of having readers test a draft document, reviewing their feedback, and revising the document in light of this feedback. Document testing is vital. It can identify problems of all kinds that even the best writers or designers miss. After you create a document, always critique it yourself and make it as good as you can. Then schedule time for testing it and receiving feedback. You may be surprised at the improvements you can still make!

There are three ways to test a document: text-based, expert-based, and user-based. The differences depend on who does the testing and what kind of feedback is given.

Text-based testing, which may be done by anyone with a good grasp of language usage, focuses on the nuts and bolts of a document—its words and sentences, its spelling, punctuation, and grammar. For example, text-based testing would determine whether a writer correctly uses the active voice, imperative mood, and parallel construction.

Expert-based testing, which is usually done by persons familiar with the procedure or mechanism described in a document, focuses on the technical accuracy of the content. These experts also check to see if supporting evidence has been included and if the document is appropriate for its intended users. Expert-based testing for a document describing how to use a Teleprompter might be carried out by a representative of the manufacturer or by persons long familiar with its use.

More Document Testing Needed

Most manufacturers tend to err on the side of doing too little rather than too much testing of computer manuals. For instance, software companies test their programs for months before release to catch every last bug, but many think nothing of putting out a manual that no one but the programmer has read and commented on. And that's a mistake. Although programmers are the best persons to catch technical errors, they may be so familiar with their programs that they fail to spot explanations that aren't detailed or clear enough for the novice user.

—Adapted from Gary Blake and Robert W. Bly, *The Elements of Technical Writing* (New York: Macmillan, 1993)

User-based testing is done by the persons for whom a document is written—the actual users of the procedure or mechanism described. Although text-based and expert-based testing can help make a document clearer and more accurate, the acid test comes when users must rely only on a document to carry out a procedure or operate a machine.

Based on what you have read, answer the following questions:

1 Why is it necessary to test a draft document?

2 Which type of document testing looks for technical accuracy?

3 Which type looks for such things as correct use of the active voice, imperative mood, and parallel construction?

4 Why is user-based testing important?

Be prepared to share your answers with the class.

Feedback

Information that writers and designers receive from document testers is called feedback. The four categories of feedback are content, structural, editorial, and design. Each type of test may produce all four categories of feedback, but each type usually focuses on one or two categories.

Content feedback relates to the information contained in a document. For example, someone might ask,

- Is the information accurate?
- Is the information complete?
- Is any information confusing?
- Is any information unnecessary?
- Is the content appropriate for the audience and purpose?

This category of feedback is best provided by expert-based testing, though nonexperts who are familiar with the subject matter might also detect problems with content.

Structural feedback relates to the overall organization of a document. The tester might ask,

- Is the information chunked?
- Is the information presented in a logical order?
- Is the organization appropriate for the audience and purpose?

While user-based testing may be the best way to detect structural problems, readers other than a document's likely users might also be able to give structural feedback.

Editorial feedback relates to a document's language and style. Someone might ask,

- Is the document free of spelling and punctuation errors?
- Is the document grammatically correct?
- Is the wording clear?
- Are the language and style appropriate for the audience and purpose?

This category of feedback concerns the kinds of matters involved in text-based testing.

Design feedback relates to the appearance of a document. The reviewer may ask,

- Are the information chunks labeled and separated by white space?
- Do the graphic devices, color, and shading create coherence and establish emphasis?
- Do the textual, spatial, and graphic elements improve the document's persuasiveness and clarity?
- Is the document's overall appearance appealing?
- Are the verbal and visual elements effectively coordinated?

This category of feedback is mainly the concern of text-based testing, though user-based testing can also contribute.

> ***"The difficulty is not to affect your reader, but to affect him precisely as you wish."***
>
> —Robert Louis Stevenson, Scottish poet and novelist

Based on what you have read, answer the following questions:

1 What are the four categories of feedback obtained by testing a draft document?

2 Which two categories of feedback are concerned with the chunking of information?

3 Which two categories of feedback are best obtained through text-based testing?

4 Which types of testing are capable of producing all four categories of feedback?

Be prepared to share your answers with the class.

Revising

From the four categories of feedback come four categories of revision that a document must undergo before it is finished. These categories are content revision, structural revision, editorial revision, and design revision.

Content feedback leads to revision that makes a document more accurate, complete, clear, and concise.

Structural feedback leads to revision ensuring that the information is chunked and presented in a logical order.

Editorial feedback leads to revision that rids a document of errors in spelling, punctuation, and grammar. It also improves the document's clarity.

Design feedback leads to revision that ensures the labeling and separation of information chunks, as well as coherence and appropriate emphasis. It helps improve a document's persuasiveness, clarity, and overall appearance.

Based on what you have read, answer the following questions:

1. What are the goals in making content revisions?
2. What are the goals in making structural revisions?
3. What are the goals in making editorial revisions?
4. What are the goals in making design revisions?

Be prepared to share your answers with the class.

A Language Checklist

Use the following checklist when you revise your document for language:

- ☐ Use active verbs when possible.
- ☐ Vary sentence types.
- ☐ Emphasize important words through placement.
- ☐ Be specific.
- ☐ Eliminate wordiness.
- ☐ Use parallel structure.
- ☐ Use headings to organize your document.
- ☐ Avoid trite and slang expressions.
- ☐ Avoid a very fancy or formal style of language.

—Adapted from Arthur H. Bell, *Business Communication: Toward 2000* (Cincinnati: South-Western, 1992)

Trying It Out

This Is Only a Test

To improve the textual and technical accuracy of your instructions and mechanism description, as well as their appeal to your intended readers, you need to get all four categories of feedback. The best way to do this is to conduct a test that covers all three testing types: text-based, expert-based, and user-based.

> ***"To write simply is as difficult as to be good."***
>
> —W. Somerset Maugham,
> English novelist and playwright

Ask a classmate to read and critique the instructions you have designed. Your classmate should use a copy of the **Document Feedback** form (page 94) to evaluate your work. At the same time, you should use another copy of the form to read and critique your classmate's document.

You will note that the form asks for all four categories of feedback. At this point, you and your classmates have not only learned how to write and design instructions but have also become familiar with the Teleprompter or another mechanism. So you are entitled to consider yourselves qualified to critique each other's documents from the expert's and the user's viewpoints, as well as on the basis of editorial quality and design.

When both of you have completed the form, carefully study your classmate's critique. Also review the self-critique you performed at the beginning of this lesson. Then, on a separate sheet of paper, list the changes you feel you should make in revising your document.

Be prepared to discuss your proposed changes in class.

Summing Up

One More Go at It

Now it's time to do a final revision of your document on the computer. In most cases, it is advisable to do content revision first—changing the order, wording, or design of a passage whose content may be changed or dropped is a waste of time. Then proceed to make structural, editorial, and design revisions.

Save your final draft. Print out a hard copy of your final draft, and keep it in your portfolio with your first draft.

Be prepared to share your final draft with the class.

ACTIVITY FORM

Document Feedback

Writer ______________________ Reader ______________________

Category	Reviewer Questions	Yes	No	Suggestions for Improvement
Content	Is the information accurate?			
	Is the information complete?			
	Is any information confusing?			
	Is any information unnecessary?			
	Is the content appropriate for the audience and purpose?			
Structural	Is the information chunked?			
	Are the instructional steps presented in a logical order?			
	Is the organization appropriate for the audience and purpose?			
Editorial	Is the document free of spelling and punctuation errors?			
	Is the document grammatically correct?			
	Are the active voice, imperative mood, and parallel construction used in giving instructions?			
	Is the wording clear?			
	Are the language and style appropriate for the audience and purpose?			
Design	Are the information chunks labeled and separated by white space?			
	Do the graphic devices, color, and shading create coherence and establish emphasis?			
	Do the textual, spatial, and graphic elements improve the document's persuasiveness and clarity?			
	Is the document's overall appearance appealing?			
	Are the verbal and visual elements effectively co-ordinated?			

Keeping Track

On a separate sheet of paper, answer the following questions. Use what you have learned in this lesson to help you.

1. What are three methods for assessing the accuracy and appeal of documents? Briefly explain each one.

2. In testing documents, what are four categories of feedback sought from readers? Briefly explain each one.

3. What is the main purpose or goal of receiving this feedback, and why is it important?

When "Correct" Is Wrong

There are a number of ways that a "correct" procedure may be misunderstood. One occurs when the procedure assumes knowledge that the procedure user does not possess. Suppose a procedure writer instructs users to start a pump but does not include instructions to check for abnormal vibration. Now assume that this procedure is executed by a novice user who fails to check for vibration and that the pump is in fact faulty; as a result, an expensive pump is damaged. The user may argue that the procedure was not correct because it omitted instructions to check for vibration, while the procedure writer may argue that the user should have known to do that.

Obviously, in situations such as these, arguments over whether the procedure was "correct" are moot; the procedure was not executed successfully, and that is what matters.

—Adapted from Douglas Wieringa, Christopher Moore, and Valerie Barnes, *Procedure Writing: Principles and Practices* (Columbus, OH: Battelle Press, 1993)

Going Further

- If you designed a Teleprompter document, contact an executive at a nearby TV station. Make arrangements for expert-based testing on your document by an employee at the station who is familiar with Teleprompter operation. Either in person or by mail, show the employee a copy of your document, and have the Teleprompter operator fill out a blank copy of the **Document Feedback** form. After the form is completed, write a paragraph stating how you would need to revise your document to take into account this expert's feedback. Be prepared to turn in your work to your teacher and to discuss what you learned with the class.

- Find a document giving instructions for the operation of a household gadget—perhaps a can opener, smoke alarm, or TV remote control—that you do not know how to use. Try to operate the mechanism by following the manufacturer's instructions. Then, using a blank copy of the **Document Feedback** form, provide user-based feedback. Write a paragraph describing the accuracy and appeal of the instructions. Be prepared to turn in your work to your teacher.

- Contact the personnel office of a local factory whose products require operating instructions. Find out who writes these instructions and, with your teacher's permission, invite this person to speak to your class about how the instructions are tested.

"Whoever wants to accomplish great things must devote a lot of profound thought to details."

—Paul Valéry, French writer

LESSON 11

Learning about Proposals

A Concept Lesson

Looking Ahead

What This Lesson Is About

In this lesson, you will learn about proposals—what they are, why they are necessary, and how to write them. You will discover that persuasive writing is essential if you want to create an effective proposal. In addition, you will learn how to write a process description, because proposals often contain one or more of these.

Internal proposals are written by individuals within an organization and are then submitted to supervisors or managers. These proposals usually recommend solutions to internal problems. External proposals are submitted to outside funding sources or prospective customers. These proposals may request grants for new projects, or they may offer to sell a product or provide a service for a certain fee.

To be effective, a proposal must be persuasive. It must recognize the needs of the reader, establish the credibility of the proposer, develop a logical case for adopting the proposed plan, and present a justifiable budget for carrying out the plan.

Most proposals include process descriptions to explain how the plan will be scheduled, implemented, and assessed. Some proposals also include instructions and mechanism descriptions.

Where the money goes

Percent of grant dollars, 1995*

12% Arts and humanities
17% Health
5% Environment and animals
5% Science and technology
4% International affairs
2% Social science
2% Religion
12% Public/society benefit**
17% Human services
25% Education

*Figures do not equal 100% because of rounding.
**Includes civil rights and social action, community improvement, philanthropy and voluntarism, and public affairs.

Source: *Foundation Giving, 1997,* published by the Foundation Center

Key Ideas

persauasive—having the power to convince other people to do or believe something; in a proposal, persuasiveness takes the form of a logical argument based on facts and sound reasoning

proposal—a persuasive document suggesting a solution to a problem or need

Request for Proposals (RFP)—a formal announcement or notice that funds are available to organizations that can provide specific services or products; a request lists the requirements that proposals must meet, the deadline for submitting proposals, and the place where they must be sent

Does Your Voice Change?

Think of two different situations in which you are asking for something or recommending a change. One situation should be informal, such as asking a friend to let you borrow her car. The other situation should be formal, such as asking the city street commissioner to install a traffic light at an intersection where several young children cross the street on their way to school. (In this type of situation, pretend that you represent a group of concerned citizens.) In both cases, your goal is to persuade someone to grant your request. However, the way you approach a friend and the way you approach a public official or an organization may be quite different.

On a sheet of paper, make two columns by drawing a line down the middle. At the top of one column, write a brief description of your informal situation and the request you want to make. At the top of the other column, do the same with your formal situation and request. Then answer the following questions about each situation. Write your responses in the appropriate columns.

1. What form would you use for your request or recommendation—a note, a memo, a letter, or a formal report? (For the purposes of this activity, assume that both requests must be in writing.)
2. How long would your request be?

3 In presenting your information and request, would you use the first-person (I, we) or the third-person (the students of XYZ School) point of view?

4 How much would you need to know about the needs and viewpoints of the individual (or organization) receiving your request? How much should that party know about you or the group you represent?

Now decide how you would summarize the similarities and differences of the two situations and how your presentation might differ in each case.

Be prepared to discuss your conclusions with the class.

Getting Started

What Is a Proposal?

In simplest terms, a proposal offers to provide goods or services or recommends a change in procedures or policies. It is accompanied by an offer to assist in bringing about the change.

A proposal may offer to solve a problem, investigate a subject, or sell a product or service. However, its approach is always persuasive. Proposals present information chiefly to convince the reader that a problem exists, that the proposed approach is valid, and that the writer or the writer's organization is qualified to do the job. In short, a proposal says, "This is what we need to know (or need to do), and this is how I (or we) can help to fill that need."

Types. Proposals come in a variety of types and sizes:

- **External proposals** are written by individuals or organizations that have a product, a service, or an idea to sell. An external proposal may be a contractor's bid for remodeling an apartment building or a nonprofit agency's request for funding to support an after-school program for teenagers. The reader may be a foundation, a corporation, or a government agency, or it may be an individual or a business that plans to issue a contract for services. Depending on the funding source and the amount of the grant request, external proposals may be 25 to 200 pages long, including attachments.

- **Internal proposals** are written by individuals within a company or organization. These proposals usually suggest changes in procedures or rules. An internal proposal may suggest a way of recruiting employees, outline a training program for new employees, or suggest a change in hours for the cafeteria. Internal proposals do not usually request funds. They are often less formal in language and

The Informal Letter Proposal

Letter proposals are informal, can be brief (usually two to five pages), and contain information about the project plan, staffing, and budget. They may also include a brief statement that requests a positive step—for example, asking the reader to sign the letter as authorization to begin work.

—Gary Blake and Robert W. Bly, *The Elements of Technical Writing* (New York: Macmillan, 1993) structure than external proposals. Informal proposals may be as brief as a one-page memo or, for more complex projects, as long as nine or ten pages.

- **Solicited proposals** are written in response to an invitation from a funding source or some other party. Sometimes a formal Request for Proposals (RFP) is issued; however, proposals may also be solicited informally, such as when a manager invites employees to submit ideas for solving a problem.
- **Unsolicited proposals** are not written in response to an invitation. The individual or the organization that has identified some problem or need initiates such proposals.

Persuasiveness. All proposals are persuasive in nature. Whether you are proposing a change in lunch-hour schedules or presenting a plan to provide services to homeless people at a cost of $1 million a year, your proposal's success will depend on your ability to be persuasive. You must convince the decision maker who reads it that your plan is necessary, that it will provide certain benefits, that you are capable of conducting the project, and that the cost of carrying out the plan is reasonable. To accomplish this, you must know how to be persuasive.

To write persuasively, you must understand the needs of your reader, you must come across as a qualified and credible person, and you must present a logical argument.

REQUEST FOR PROPOSALS

1998 Water and Watersheds Research

This is part of an interagency research program involving EPA, NSF, and USDA. The program emphasizes well-integrated, interdisciplinary, fundamental or applied research on important scientific, engineering, and social principles for understanding, protecting, and restoring water resources and watershed processes in the U.S. and other regions of the world. A systems approach and general applicability of the research to watershed-scale questions are required in each proposal. The emphasis for 1998 will be on research that considers restoration and rehabilitation of damaged or degraded systems.

Deadline: April 1, 1998

—Mid-Atlantic Region Sea Grant (http://www.mdsg.umd.edu/Jobs/index.html#RFP)

LET'S KEEP IT CLEAN!

Attention all park employees and visitors: Lake Blackwood has been revitalized and cleaned up over the last few years, but we need ideas on how to keep it that way. How can we best utilize our resources to maintain the beauty of the lake? Please submit your proposals to me at the administration office, or via e-mail (elwisty@blackwood.net).

—E. L. Wisty, Park Administrator

A Request for Proposals (RFP), such as the sample above, is a formal document that was issued to solicit proposals for a specific project. The poster at right, though an informal document, can also be an effective way to generate new ideas and proposals.

1. **Understand and acknowledge your readers' needs.** The first step in persuading someone to accept a proposal is to make sure that the need or problem that the proposal addresses is relevant to your reader. For example, if you would like to propose selling typewriter ribbons to a company, make sure the firm has not replaced all its electric typewriters with personal computers. Before you submit a proposal to the purchasing department, you should learn as much as you can about the company: inquire about its equipment; find out what types of customers it serves; read the company profile.

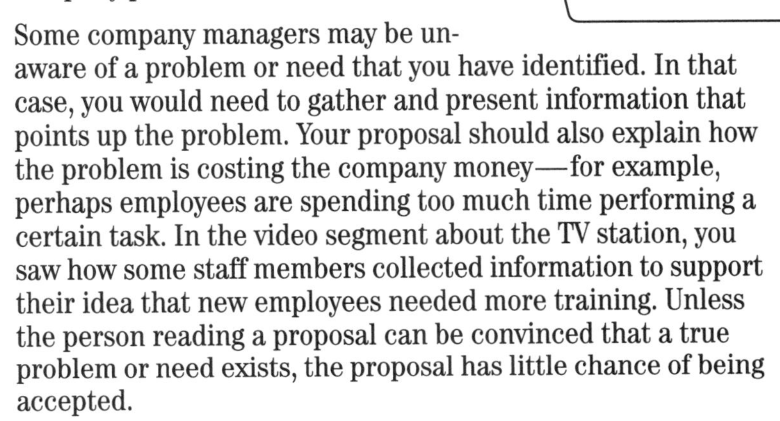

   Some company managers may be unaware of a problem or need that you have identified. In that case, you would need to gather and present information that points up the problem. Your proposal should also explain how the problem is costing the company money—for example, perhaps employees are spending too much time performing a certain task. In the video segment about the TV station, you saw how some staff members collected information to support their idea that new employees needed more training. Unless the person reading a proposal can be convinced that a true problem or need exists, the proposal has little chance of being accepted.

2. **Establish your credibility.** In addition to convincing a decision maker that your plan should be implemented, you must also convince this person that you or your organization is best qualified to do the work. This means citing your credentials: include a summary of your training and experience; describe similar projects that you completed successfully; perhaps even provide some references (names of other people in the field) who can attest to your competence. This will give anyone who reads the proposal good reasons to believe in you and your organization. The proposal itself will boost your credibility if it shows that you understand the problem, that you have a well-planned course of action and a reasonable budget, and that you have taken the pains to produce a well-written and well-designed document.

3. **Present your argument logically.** All recommendations in your proposal must be based on accurate facts and sound assumptions. First, establish that a problem or need exists. Then explain how you will deal with it. To do this, list your objectives, show how each one is directly related to the problem, and demonstrate how your proposal will accomplish the objectives and will benefit your audience. To be persuasive, your argument should develop in a clear, convincing way. Each part of your proposal "speaks" to every other part. The parts build on one another in a logical progression. (This idea is developed in Lesson 12.)

> ***"If you have an important point to make, don't try to be subtle or clever. Use a pile driver. Hit the point once. Then come back and hit it again. Then a third time—a tremendous whack."***
>
> —Winston Churchill, British statesman and writer

Using what you have read, answer the following questions:

1 How are internal and external proposals similar and different?

2 What is a solicited proposal?

3 What are the three elements of effective persuasion?

Be prepared to share your answers with the class.

Describing Processes

To give a reader a clear picture of how a plan will work, it is often necessary for the proposal writer to describe one or more processes. How the project will be carried out, how it will be scheduled over time, and how it will be evaluated are three processes that may need to be described.

A process description provides a general overview. It defines the process and identifies its purpose or goal. It also lists the sequence of steps in the process. The purpose and effect of each step should be clearly described.

The following example of a process description is from a proposal written by Aimee, a young woman working as a farmhand at Green Visions, Inc., a large corporate farm. From her experience in the Future Farmers of America chapter at her school, Aimee learned about the value of establishing "buffer strips" along the banks of rivers and creeks. These narrow strips of land are dedicated to grasses instead of crops. When Green Visions purchased 1,000 acres of new land, Aimee decided to approach the owners with a

Putting the Brakes on Disappearing Dirt

In the United States, current estimates of on-site productivity losses from erosion range from $500 million to $18 billion per year. The costs for off-site environmental problems range from $2 billion to $8 billion per year. The United States Soil Conservation Service estimates that almost half of the arable land in the U.S. is afflicted by "excessive" rates of erosion. One technique to combat soil degradation is to reserve highly erodible soil for agricultural production that does not involve tillage or plowing.

—Adapted from William Bender and Margaret Smith, "Population, Food, and Nutrition," *Population Bulletin* (February 1997)

plan to establish buffer strips. After stating the potential benefits of such strips, she presented the following description of the process needed to create them.

Aimee's Process Description

Planting buffer strips would benefit Green Vision's image and financial outlook by reducing soil erosion, beautifying the farm, and providing a wildlife corridor. What's more, doing so is a reasonably easy task, given our present equipment and the expertise of our staff. What we need to do is:

- **Measuring**—Our field runs along Wapsy Creek for about 150 yards. The ideal width for the strips could be determined by Chris or another supervisor, keeping in mind that the wider the strip, the better the protection.
- **Planting**—Assuming that a 20-foot width on both sides of the stream is the most we can spare, the planting area would be 18,000 square feet. Virtually any grass seed, available from local agricultural-supply dealers, will work well on the buffer strips.
- **Maintaining**—Using a standard grass seed will hold maintenance costs to the minimum, because only bald sections will need to be replanted. In addition, the strips should be left unmowed and periodically burned off to promote growth. Buffer strips, therefore, represent basically a one-time expense to protect Green Vision's property for years.

> ***"Keep in mind the better you understand what you want and why you want it, the better your chances will be of acquiring it."***
>
> —Fred Jandt, *Win-Win Negotiating*, 1985

Although the structure of a process description is similar to that of a set of directions or instructions (described in Lesson 6), some key differences exist:

- Process descriptions are less detailed than directions. They are not intended to be complete enough for someone to carry out the steps without additional information.
- Process descriptions are written in the indicative mood rather than the imperative. (Indicative mood: "Using a standard grass seed will hold maintenance costs to the minimum"; imperative mood: "Use a standard grass seed to hold maintenance costs to the minimum."
- Because process descriptions focus on the process itself rather than the person conducting it, they tend to use the passive voice instead of the active. (Passive voice: "the strips should be left unmowed and periodically burned off to promote growth"; active voice: "To promote growth, we should not mow the strips, though periodically we should burn them off.")

Internal Proposals

Internal proposals are quite simply those that remain within the writer's organization. They are usually directed to a specific individual, department, or functional area. They range in formality from handwritten suggestion-box entries to lengthy reports. An internal proposal may be a brief suggestion submitted to an immediate supervisor or a departmental project designed to persuade the Chief Executive Officer (CEO) to authorize the development of a new product line.

—Adapted from Joel P. Bowman and Bernadine P. Branchaw, *How to Write Proposals That Produce* (Phoenix: Oryx, 1992)

Using what you have read, answer the following questions:

1. How are process descriptions different from instructions?
2. What sections of a proposal are most likely to contain process descriptions?
3. What is the reason for using the imperative mood in instructions but not in process descriptions?

Be prepared to share your answers with the class.

Trying It Out

Educating Pet Owners

In Lesson 8, Jennifer Albert, a veterinary technician, redesigned the postoperative instructions for Raintree Animal Hospital. Those instructions turned out to be a big help to people who brought their pets to the hospital. Jennifer and an associate, José Sandoz, have come to the conclusion that a much broader educational-outreach effort is needed, not only to reduce post-surgical complications but also to provide information about nutrition, accident prevention, and behavioral problems.

Unfortunately, the veterinarians who own the hospital are swamped with work. Recently the city council decided to subsidize the cost of neutering dogs and cats that people bring to the city's animal shelter for placement in other homes. This has nearly doubled the number of ovariohysterectomies (spayings) and orchiectomies (castrations) that the hospital performs. As a result, the vets have been too busy to think about an outreach program, and so Jennifer and José have put together a proposal.

All-American Pets

According to the *U.S. Pet Ownership and Demographics Sourcebook,* billions of dollars are spent on cats and dogs for veterinary care. Some 34.6 million households own dogs, and 29.2 million households own cats. Of the total pet population, 52.6 million are dogs and 57.5 million are cats. In households obtaining vet care, 82 percent need vet care for their dogs, while 62 percent need it for cats.

Proposal for Expanded Educational Programming by Raintree Animal Hospital

Submitted to

G. R. Growley, VMD, and Ling Fu Mu, VMD

by

Jennifer Albert and José Sandoz, Veterinary Technicians

Introduction

The sudden increase in the number of ovariohysterectomies and orchiectomies performed at the Raintree Animal Hospital since the passage of City Council Ordinance K-9 underscores the need for intensified outreach and educational programming by the hospital staff. As demonstrated by the rise in postsurgical complications, the new clients we are seeing are, on the whole, less experienced and less knowledgeable about pet care than our regular clientele. Many are first-time pet owners; others are older people who are not aware of current nutritional standards for animals or the risks of allowing pets to roam freely. Many of those we see in the clinic are recent immigrants from Mexico and South America, with a limited command of English.

This increase in the volume of business offers both an exciting opportunity and a serious threat to the hospital. The new owners of the animals that the shelter has referred to us for neutering under the council's subsidy program are potential long-term clients, especially if they are made aware of the need for regular check-ups, vaccinations, and grooming. They may also decide to use the hospital's boarding services. However, if these owners do not receive adequate training in pet care, there is a risk that the hospital's postoperative complication rates and other preventable health problems among its patients may grow excessive, damaging the hospital's reputation as a provider of high-quality health care.

Raintree Animal Hospital enjoys a long-standing reputation for quality and economical services. We understand that your goal, as owners, is to see the hospital grow into a full-service veterinary center for household pets from throughout the tri-state region. To reinforce this reputation for excellence and to enhance the potential for controlled, continuous expansion, we are presenting the following proposal for a comprehensive educational-outreach program.

The Plan

We propose to establish and conduct a multifaceted educational-outreach program to help pet owners at various levels learn more about preventive and follow-up care for their household animals. The effort would range from simple handouts, such as the instructions for postoperative care, to presentations at churches and community meetings and to hands-on workshops where owners would practice techniques for managing difficult pets and reducing aggressive behavior. We also propose to hold semiannual "well-pet" clinics where animals could receive check-ups and rabies shots and where their owners could obtain informative literature about animal care.

Potential Benefits

Potential benefits of this initiative include

- increased exposure for the hospital and its staff among pet owners and potential pet owners throughout the tri-state area—exposure that translates into both goodwill and increased use of our services.
- fewer postoperative complications and preventable injuries and illnesses among the hospital's patients, thereby enhancing its reputation for high-quality care.
- greater cooperation with area animal shelters, which may see increases in adoptions as residents become more aware of available services and gain confidence in their ability to care for pets.
- improved relationships with local officials as the city council sees strong, private-sector support for the new ordinance and as animal-control officers deal with fewer violations because pet owners will be more aware of local regulations and the need to restrain household pets.
- possible recognition for the hospital and its veterinarians from such organizations as the chamber of commerce, which gives annual community-service awards, and the local humane society, which honors those who contribute to the well-being of animals.

Approach

In discussing our approach to this plan, we will consider methodology, management, qualifications, budget, and schedule.

Methodology—The proposed initiative consists of four stages:

Stage 1—Speakers Bureau. Following a brainstorming session among the hospital's veterinary professionals, approximately 10 topics would be identified for the initial offering through the speakers bureau, and appropriate staff would be assigned to develop a 15-minute presentation on each topic. (These topics may include such areas as nutrition and safety, prevention and treatment of common health problems, bathing and grooming, behavior management, the benefits of pet therapy, children and pets, etc.) The resources available through the speakers bureau could be publicized in a letter and flyer sent to community organizations, schools, service clubs, and churches throughout the region. Information on how to schedule a speaker would be provided, and recipients would be invited to suggest additional topics. In addition, a special mailing would go to all newspapers and radio and television stations in the area, offering to make available informed spokespersons who could respond to breaking news stories involving small animals and household pets.

Stage 2—Workshops. As an extension of the speakers bureau, five workshops in community settings would be scheduled for the first year. Staff would also brainstorm ideas for the workshop sessions, which may cover many of the same topics as the speakers bureau, though in greater detail and with the opportunity for hands-on training. For example, a speaker might discuss the general principles of obedience training for young dogs, while a workshop might include several sessions in which training techniques can be demonstrated and owners can practice the techniques with their dogs. Another workshop might include pet-sitting training for teenagers who care for pets. In some cases, a small registration fee for the workshops could be charged to cover the cost of materials and rental space.

Stage 3—Instructional Materials. Materials for use as handouts at the workshops would also be available to hospital clients at the registration counter. These materials would be designed for readability, with the target audience in mind. For example, some could be printed in large type for older persons with vision limitations, and some could be printed in Spanish for those with limited fluency in English.

Stage 4—Special Clinics. Periodic vaccination and "well pet" clinics would be scheduled. The number of clinics may be based on the level of interest shown at speaking engagements and workshops. The cost of vaccines may be subsidized by the county health department or by private organizations.

Management—Jennifer Albert and José Sandoz are prepared to coordinate the planning of the educational-outreach initiative. Preliminary discussion with other staff members indicates that most of the employees would be willing to volunteer as speakers or workshop coordinators. We would look to the veterinary physicians—whose time, we realize, is limited—for guidance, direction, and occasional presentations. The animal shelter's auxiliary has also expressed interest in helping with this initiative. Some of those volunteers may be trained as speakers, while others may assist with workshops and clinics.

Qualifications—Albert and Sandoz are experienced veterinary technicians. Both have worked at Raintree Animal Hospital for more than five years. They demonstrated their commitment to client education by proposing and producing the successful postoperative-care instructions. Albert, who holds a communications degree as well as vet-tech certification, could produce the educational and publicity materials on the hospital's desktop-publishing equipment. Sandoz, whose native language is Spanish, could translate all handouts for the Latino population. Because the doctors and other professional staff members are active in various community organizations, they could help spread word of the programs. Other staff members have volunteered to perform clerical tasks, make arrangements, handle phone calls, and photograph or videotape events.

Budget—Costs for implementing the proposed plan would be minimal because the plan would be based on the volunteer efforts of the hospital's staff and friends. Some expenses for postage, copies, and rent may be incurred; however, the increased business that the hospital stands to gain should far exceed these modest costs.

Schedule—Planning will begin immediately upon notification that this proposal has been approved. The speakers bureau could be fully operational within two months from that date. The first workshop would be held within three months. The first clinic would take place in early spring (if funding is available).

Evaluation

Everyone who participates in a workshop and all members of the audience at a speaking engagement would be invited to complete a brief evaluation form. These forms could be analyzed over time to assess the effectiveness of various presenters and the level of interest in the different topics.

In addition, the referral source for all new clients would be monitored, and the number of clients who learned about the clinic through one of the outreach initiatives would be recorded monthly to gauge the effect on client recruitment. Other strategies for measuring the effectiveness of the educational sessions could be explored and implemented.

Conclusion

This proposal is submitted out of concern for the future of Raintree Animal Hospital, as well as for the health and well-being of the small animals in the region it serves. We believe that this effort can be conducted at a minimal cost, without detracting from the assigned work of the staff. Indeed, we believe that this group effort can contribute to the improvement of staff morale and serve as a vehicle for developing the staff's creativity, presentation skills, and public-relations expertise.

We look forward to hearing your reaction to our proposal, and we will be glad to respond to any questions you may have. We hope that you will share our enthusiasm for engaging in educational outreach.

Using what you have learned in this lesson, answer the following questions about Jennifer and José's proposal:

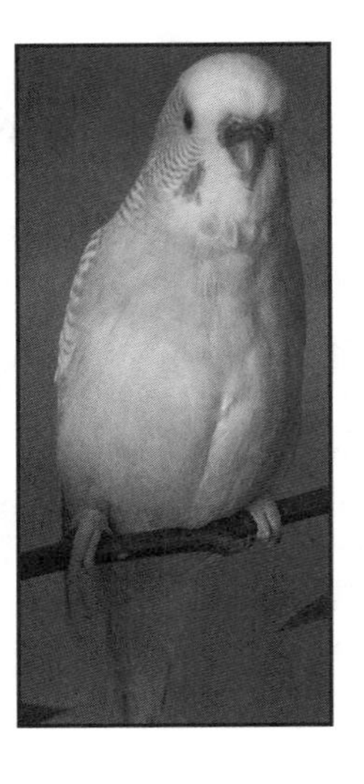

1. What is the purpose of the proposal?
2. Is it an internal or external proposal? Explain.
3. Is it a solicited or unsolicited proposal? How do you know?
4. What needs of the reader does the proposal acknowledge?
5. How do the proposers (Jennifer and José) show that they are qualified to do the work?
6. Is the argument logical? Explain your response.
7. Does this proposal contain a process description? If so, what process is described?

Be prepared to share your answers with the class.

Vet-Tech Tasks

Veterinary technicians and technologists

- perform medical tests for use in the diagnosis and treatment of diseases in animals.
- prepare vaccines and serums for prevention of diseases.
- take blood samples and prepare tissue samples.
- conduct laboratory tests such as urinalysis and blood counts.
- clean and sterilize instruments and materials.
- maintain equipment.

—Adapted from *Occupational Outlook Handbook*, 1996–97 ed., U.S. Department of Labor (January 1996)

Summing Up

What Is Your Response?

Imagine that you are Dr. Growley or Dr. Mu. You have just read Jennifer and José's proposal and answered the preceding questions. Your waiting room is full of people and animals, you have a full surgical schedule this week, and you have been working until 8 p.m. every day. You are not convinced the plan can work unless you give it a lot of your time (which you don't have) or unless you hire another staff person (which you can't afford). You appreciate the enthusiasm and the willingness of the staff, but you are not sure they have thought through all aspects of the plan in a complete and realistic way.

Draft a memo to Jennifer and José. Express your appreciation for their ideas and for their effort in writing the proposal. Then raise any questions they have failed to address in their proposal. Finally, give them your decision. Come up with an answer of your own, or use one of these:

"I will give you my response after I hear your answers to the questions I have raised."

"Thanks but no thanks. We don't have time to do this now."

"It's a great idea, but let's take it one step at a time, starting with the speakers bureau. Then we'll decide whether to go on with the rest."

Be prepared to share your response with the class—and to defend it, if necessary.

Keeping Track

On a separate sheet of paper, respond to the following. Use what you have learned in this lesson to help you.

1. Give at least three characteristics of internal proposals and at least three characteristics of external proposals.
2. What are the three elements of persuasion?
3. How do process descriptions differ from instructions?

Going Further

- Identify someone in your school or community who receives proposals from other people. Perhaps your principal or dean receives internal proposals suggesting changes within the school. Or if there is a charitable foundation in your area, call and ask to speak to a program officer. Tell this person that you are learning to write proposals and that you would like to know what someone who reads proposals wants to see in them. Also ask what criteria are used in deciding whether to accept a request. Ask for a copy of the guidelines for submitting proposals and a copy of a proposal that was approved. Summarize what you learn in a one- or two-page paper, and turn in your report to your teacher. With your teacher's permission, invite the person you interviewed to visit your class and to share his or her ideas.

- Many government agencies and a number of national foundations have sites on the World Wide Web that include requests for proposals. You can often download a copy of the RFP onto your computer and complete it. Imagine that you need to respond to an RFP found in one of the sites listed in "RFP Express" on this page. Download or print out the RFP, and compare its sections with the sections in the outreach proposal you just read. How is it similar, and in what ways is it different? Identify any sections in the on-line RFP that might be difficult to complete. Write a one-page report summarizing your findings. Be prepared to share your report and the on-line RFP form with the class.

RFP Express

Look at the following Web sites for announcements of RFPs and helpful information on completing proposals.

- American Communication Association Grants and Fellowships page (http://www.uark.edu/depts/comminfo/www/grants.html)
- The World Wide Web Virtual Library, IANWeb Resources (http://ian.vse.cz/resource/grants.htm)
- Pitsco's Launch to Grants and Funding (http://www.pitsco.com/pitsco/grants.html)
- Nonprofit Resources Catalogue, grants and funding sources (http://www.clark.net/pub/pwalker/Fundraising_and_Giving/)
- Federally Funded Research Projects (http://medoc.gdb.org/best/fedfund.html)

- Working alone or in a small group, identify a problem at your school. Perhaps the cafeteria is too crowded, or maybe there's not enough time between classes for students to walk from one end of the campus to the other. Find some problem or school policy that causes inconvenience for some students. Then come up with a solution. Using what you have learned in this lesson, write a proposal to the most appropriate person (the principal, the athletic director, the cafeteria manager, or any other official). Make sure that you describe the problem clearly and that you present your solution in a persuasive way. Be prepared to turn in your proposal to your teacher—and perhaps to send it to the appropriate person at your school.

LESSON 12

Writing a Proposal

A Strategies Lesson

Looking Ahead

What This Lesson Is About

In this lesson, you will learn about the various components of a proposal. You will also see how a flowchart can be used as an aid to planning. Using what you have learned, you will then create an internal proposal.

- Although companies and foundations often have their own guidelines for preparing proposals, most proposals answer these basic questions: What is the problem? What is your plan to resolve it? What are the expected benefits? How will you carry out the plan? How are you qualified to do so? What will the costs be? How will you know that your plan is successful?
- These questions are answered in various sections of a proposal. All the sections should be interrelated and should "talk to each other."
- In internal proposals, some of the sections may be combined, the tone may be quite informal, and the writer may use the first person in presenting information and opinions.

Key Ideas

evaluation—assessment; measurement of accomplishment

objectives—aims, goals

Build Your Case!

Think of a situation in which you want to persuade somebody to do something. The "something" might be to lend you a car, to vote for a candidate, or to change a rule that you consider unfair. In your journal, briefly describe the situation and what you want. Then build your case. State the problem or need and the benefits of correcting it. Describe your plan, project how much the plan will cost, and explain how you are qualified to carry it out.

Be prepared to share your journal entry with the class.

Getting Started

What Should a Proposal Contain?

You may not have realized it, but when you wrote your case, you actually wrote a mini-proposal. You stated the problem, proposed a plan to solve it, estimated the cost, and explained how you are qualified to carry out the plan. Those are the essential ingredients of any proposal—whether you are writing it to submit to your supervisor or to a major foundation with a request for a million-dollar grant.

> "That writer does the most, who gives his reader the most knowledge, and takes from him the least time."
> —Charles Caleb Colton, English writer and clergyman

How a proposal is organized and the various parts it contains will depend on several factors:

- whether it is internal or external, formal or informal, solicited or unsolicited
- whether you are proposing a change in procedure or policy or requesting funds to carry out a project
- whether the reader (your own company or organization, or the corporation or foundation you are approaching) has specific guidelines for structuring proposals

If you are responding to a Request for Proposals (RFP) that contains an outline to follow, or if your company has a standard format for internal proposals, you should follow those guidelines. The instructions can be very detailed; for example, they might specify the size of font you should use, the manuscript's spacing, and the number of pages per section. You will need to pay attention to these details, because proposals may be rejected without being read simply because the format is wrong or they arrive one minute after the deadline.

Often, however—particularly with informal and unsolicited proposals—there may be no guidelines to follow. In this case, use a generic format, like the one in the flowchart on page 115. You can then be sure that you will answer the reader's most important questions. As you review the contents of the proposal outlined on the following pages, compare it

Nine Principles of Proposal Writing

1. Learn everything you can about your prospective client or the people who will evaluate your proposal.
2. Sell your ideas by fitting them into the client's needs.
3. Don't just solve the technical problem; empathize with the customer's critical needs.
4. Recognize all critical factors that evaluators use in assessing proposals.
5. Use appropriate graphics to highlight your ideas and make them easy to visualize.
6. Tailor each proposal to the needs of the specific client.
7. Anticipate and defuse objections.
8. Avoid hedging and subtlety in proposals.
9. Make a list of where key resources are located if you don't have a proposal library.

—Adapted from Gary Blake and Robert W. Bly, *The Elements of Technical Writing* (New York: Macmillan, 1993)

with this flowchart, which graphically displays the parts and their relationships.

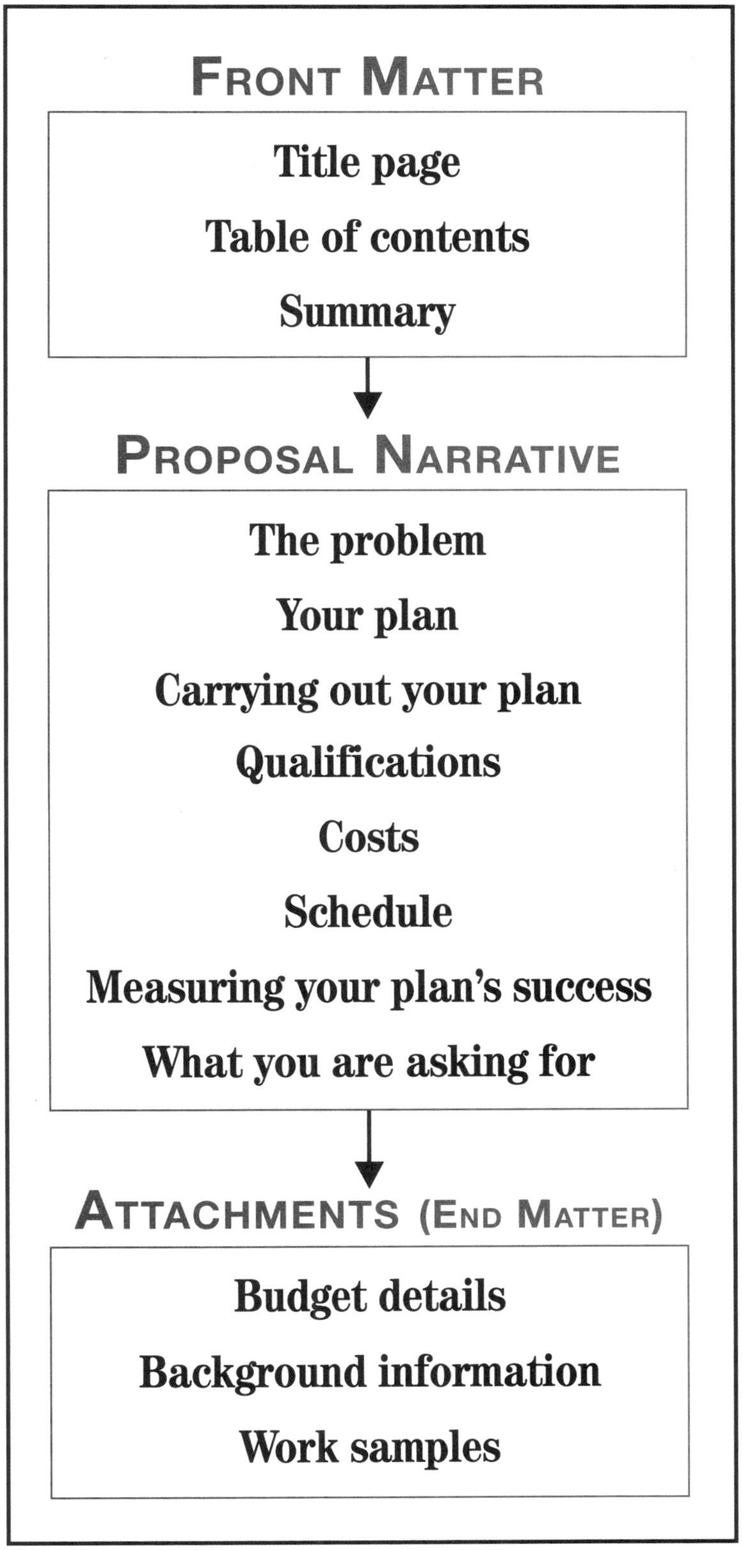

Sections of a Proposal—The following outline includes a detailed description of each section that normally makes up a formal proposal. It also shows the order in which the sections are arranged. In informal, internal proposals, many of the sections are quite short, but the key questions must be answered in any proposal.

Proposal Planning Flowchart

FRONT MATTER

- Title page
- Table of contents
- Summary

↓

PROPOSAL NARRATIVE

- The problem
- Your plan
- Carrying out your plan
- Qualifications
- Costs
- Schedule
- Measuring your plan's success
- What you are asking for

↓

ATTACHMENTS (END MATTER)

- Budget details
- Background information
- Work samples

I. Front Matter

A. **Title page.** Unless your proposal is informal and is presented as a memo or letter, you will need a title page that identifies the project, the person or organization to whom it is submitted, the name and address of the submitting organization, and the name and telephone number of a contact person (you, perhaps). Some foundations provide a form for a cover sheet, which may replace the title page.

B. **Table of contents.** A listing of each major section and the page on which it begins is necessary for longer, formal proposals but may not be needed for proposals that are only three or four pages long.

C. **Summary.** Again, this is essential for longer proposals, where the summary may be a page or more. Even in brief proposals, however, it is a good idea to summarize the request in a short paragraph or two at the beginning of the document. The summary may be all that a busy manager will read. Therefore, it should give a clear picture of what you are proposing and, at the same time, make the reader want to read the whole document. Summaries are considered in Lesson 14.

II. Proposal Narrative

The narrative is the heart of your proposal. It contains the answers to the major questions your reader will have.

A. **The problem.** In this introductory section, define the problem your proposal addresses. If the reader is not aware of the problem, present data or evidence to prove that the problem is serious and affects the reader's interests.

B. **Your plan.** State how you plan to resolve the problem (or fill the need) that you identified in the first section. List your objectives in specific, measurable terms—for example, "The project will result in a 50-percent increase in fifth-grade achievement scores in mathematics and reading." In this section, point out the benefits of taking the action you propose and the risks of not doing so. For example, if you are proposing an after-school tutoring program, you might say, "Studies show that low grades and truancy in elementary school correlate with dropping out of school prior to graduation and high rates of delinquency and later welfare dependency. Therefore, the proposed early intervention should have a positive effect not only on the students' current school performance but also on their long-term productivity as adults."

C. **Carrying out your plan.** In this section, describe the process by which you will carry out the plan. List the tasks that are involved, the people who will be responsible for performing them, and the order (or time frame) in which they will be performed. Include the number of people who will be served (if it is a service project) or the final product you are offering (if this is a sales proposal). Process descriptions are the focus of Lesson 11.

D. **Qualifications.** In this section, explain why you or your company is qualified to carry out the plan you propose. This might include a summary of major accomplishments, particularly those related to the proposed project, and a reference to résumés or other materials in the attachments.

E. **Costs.** Summarize the costs involved in carrying out the project you are proposing. If appropriate, tell how much will be saved by making the changes you suggest. With formal proposals, a detailed budget and budget narrative (explanation of each item for which funds are requested) should be attached. The narrative, however, should contain a summary of the projected costs and savings.

F. **Schedule.** Include a schedule indicating when various tasks included in the proposal will be completed.

"In writing, clarity is best achieved through the use of a simple, concise, straightforward approach."

—Kenneth T. Henson, *Writing for Successful Publication* (Bloomington, IN: National Educational Service, 1991)

G. **Measuring your plan's success.** Even brief, informal proposals usually include measures for evaluating the plan's success. In longer, more formal documents, the evaluation component includes a description of a process for monitoring and measurement. This component also requests funding for an outside evaluator to conduct the assessment.

H. **What you are asking for.** All proposals should have a conclusion in which the specific request—for a change in procedure, approval of a plan, purchase of services, or awarding of a grant—is presented. In a lengthy proposal, this may include a summary of the main points and the argument for approval or funding. In a short, informal proposal, the conclusion may be simply a final sentence in which the request is made or restated. For additional tips on wrapping up your proposal, see the sidebar on this page.

> ***"A proposal should never begin or end with a dollar sign. Conclude your proposal by expressing your willingness to help your readers. Offer to answer questions and to provide further information, to meet with or speak by phone to the evaluators, referees, or others, even to consider reshaping your proposal as necessary to meet the needs of the client or agency."***
>
> —Arthur H. Bell, *Business Communication: Toward 2000* (Cincinnati: South-Western, 1992)

III. **Attachments (End Matter)**

A. **Budget details.** Attachments may include a detailed budget for the proposed project and résumés of people who will operate it.

B. **Background information.** External proposals may include background information on the submitting organization.

C. **Work samples.** Often, samples of work similar to what is proposed in the document are included in attachments.

Although this outline presents the various sections of the proposal as separate components, they are really parts of a whole. When a proposal is well constructed, all of the parts are interrelated. In effect, they "talk" to each other. The nature of the problem determines what the outcomes (or objectives) should be. The proposed solutions are developed to accomplish the objectives. The success of the proposed solutions in achieving the objectives will be determined by the evaluation, which, in turn, will show whether the results are worth the financial investment.

Using what you have read, answer the following questions:

1 What generic questions should all proposals answer?

2 Why is a summary needed at the beginning of the proposal?

3 What items are commonly included in the attachments?

Be prepared to share your answers with the class.

Examining Jennifer and José's Proposal

Examine Jennifer and José's proposal on pages 105–109 in Lesson 11 to determine whether it contains all the key sections that a proposal should have. Remember that these sections are not always in the same order or labeled in the same way.

Be prepared to share your findings with the class.

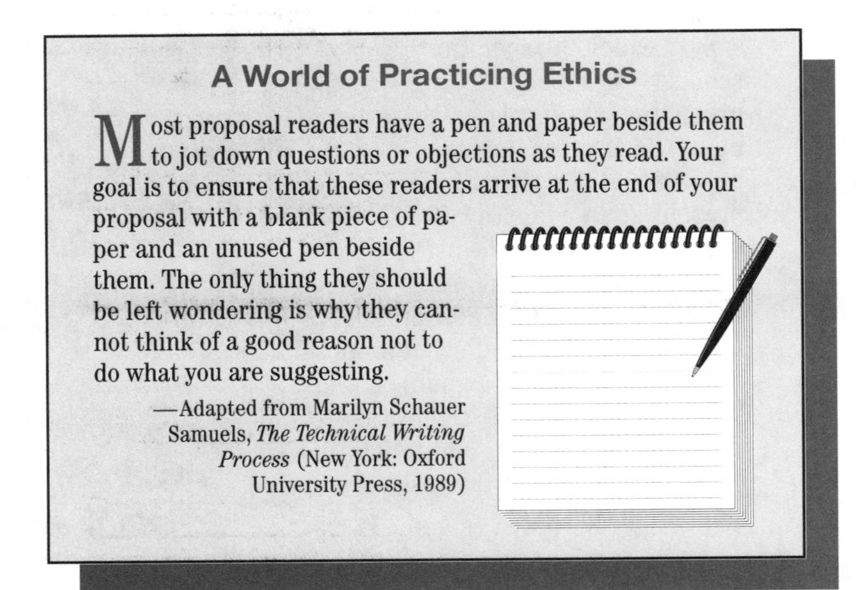

A World of Practicing Ethics

Most proposal readers have a pen and paper beside them to jot down questions or objections as they read. Your goal is to ensure that these readers arrive at the end of your proposal with a blank piece of paper and an unused pen beside them. The only thing they should be left wondering is why they cannot think of a good reason not to do what you are suggesting.

—Adapted from Marilyn Schauer Samuels, *The Technical Writing Process* (New York: Oxford University Press, 1989)

Trying It Out

Go with the Flow

If you completed the activities in Lesson 6, you used a flowchart to help you create instructions. You can also use a flowchart to help you organize your proposal. In this section, you will create an internal proposal requesting the management of Channel 3 to enhance the training and training materials available to new employees.

Review the **Proposal Planning Flowchart** on page 115. Using it as a guide and drawing on what you have learned in previous lessons, create a proposal to the operations manager at Channel 3. Start with the proposal narrative, and follow this checklist:

- ☑ State the problem. Lessons 2 and 3 explain how to identify the problem and how to support your assessment of the need.
- ☑ Briefly describe your plan for solving the problem. Identify at least two objectives for your plan. Point out the benefits of doing what you recommend, as well as the risks of not dealing with the problem.
- ☑ Describe the process by which you would carry out your plan. List the tasks and the individuals who will be

responsible for them. (For a discussion of writing process descriptions, see Lesson 11.)

- Estimate the cost of carrying out your plan.
- List your qualifications (and those of others who would work with you on the project).
- Estimate the cost of carrying out your plan.
- Include a brief schedule.
- Describe the process you will use to measure the success of your efforts.
- Write a conclusion.

Create a title page. You will need a brief summary of your proposal, and Lesson 13 will give you the opportunity to write one. The summary will go between the title page and your proposal narrative. The attachments go at the end. As attachments, include at least the sample directions and the mechanism description that you prepared in other lessons.

Remember to consider the design of your proposal. Did you use the four strategies of chunking, labeling, coherence, and emphasis?

When you have completed your proposal, take time to review it closely. Use the text-based testing techniques discussed in Lesson 10. Look for ways your document can be improved in content, structure, design, or editorial style, and make the needed changes.

Save your completed proposal, and print out two copies. Keep a copy in your portfolio. Use the other copy in the next activity to seek feedback from another student.

Reasons for Rejection

Here are seven of the most common reasons that proposals are rejected. You can use them as a checklist to make sure your proposal avoids these problems.

1. The proposer does not demonstrate a clear understanding of the problem.

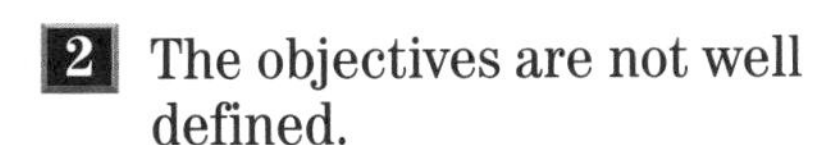

2. The objectives are not well defined.

3. The wrong audience is addressed.
4. The procedures and methodology are not specific.
5. The overall design is questionable.
6. Cost estimates are not realistic—either too high or too low.
7. Résumés of key personnel are not adequate.

—Adapted from Joel P. Bowman and Bernadine P. Branchaw, *How to Write Proposals that Produce* (Phoenix, AZ: Oryx, 1992)

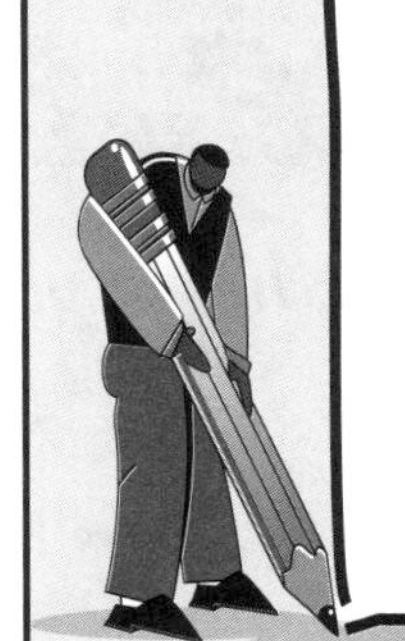

Summing Up

Getting Feedback

If you did Lesson 10, you gained valuable help in refining your instructions by asking for feedback from another student. Now you will repeat the process, this time with your proposal, which is complete except for the summary.

Exchange copies of your proposal with another student. Using a copy of page 1 of the **Proposal Review** form, review the other person's proposal. On the form, list suggestions for content improvements, while he or she reviews your proposal.

Complete page 2 of the **Proposal Review** form, and make suggestions for editorial, structural, or design improvements. Complete the overall assessment questions at the end of the form.

When you receive feedback on your proposal, make any changes that you believe will improve your document. Again, save the revision. Print out a hard copy to turn in to your teacher. You may wish to print out a second copy to keep in your portfolio.

Feedback helps you perfect your proposal.

Keeping Track

On a separate sheet of paper, answer the following questions. Use what you have learned in this lesson to help you.

1. What are the basic questions that all proposals answer?
2. What does it mean to say that the various sections of a proposal should "talk" to each other?
3. How might the format of an informal proposal differ from that of a formal one?

Proposal Review (page 1)

Your Name ______________________ Date ______________________

Review of Proposal by ______________________

	Yes	No
1. Is there a title page?	☐	☐
2. Is there a table of contents?	☐	☐
3. Is there a summary?	☐	☐
4. Does the summary reflect the content of the proposal?	☐	☐
5. Is the problem clearly stated?	☐	☐
6. Is the statement of the problem convincing?	☐	☐
7. Is the plan described?	☐	☐
8. Are objectives given?	☐	☐
9. Are objectives measurable?	☐	☐
10. Are benefits presented?	☐	☐
11. Are risks discussed?	☐	☐
12. Are the tasks listed?	☐	☐
13. Is responsibility assigned for carrying out the tasks?	☐	☐
14. Are costs provided?	☐	☐
15. Is there a schedule for implementation?	☐	☐
16. Is there an evaluation plan?	☐	☐
17. What will the evaluation plan measure?	☐	☐
18. What does the proposal ask for?	☐	☐
19. Are examples/samples attached?	☐	☐
20. Is a detailed budget included?	☐	☐

Proposal Review (page 2)

Your Name ______________________ Date ______________________

Review of Proposal by ______________________

STRUCTURAL FEEDBACK	Yes	No
1. Does the proposal follow the standard generic format?	☐	☐
2. Do the various parts "talk" to each other?	☐	☐

DESIGN FEEDBACK	Yes	No
1. Is it easy to distinguish the sections of the proposal?	☐	☐
2. Is the document attractive and inviting to the reader?	☐	☐
3. Are boldface, italics, and other highlighters used effectively?	☐	☐

EDITORIAL FEEDBACK	Yes	No
1. Is the document free of spelling, grammar, and punctuation errors?	☐	☐
2. Is the style (formal vs. informal) appropriate to the type of document and intended audience?	☐	☐
3. Is the narrative clear and concise?	☐	☐

OVERALL ASSESSMENT

1. Is the proposal persuasive? ☐ ☐

   Comment:

2. Does the proposal present a logical case for the proposed changes? ☐ ☐

   Comment:

3. If you were the operations manager, would you implement the recommendations? ☐ ☐

   Comment:

Going Further

- Imagine that you are a manager in a small company that operates in an occupational area that interests you. The company president is a strong believer in asking for and using the ideas of employees to improve the operation and the product. However, no system is in place for the employees to relay their ideas to the management. The president asks you to develop a standard format for employee suggestions—your company's own RFP. He asks you to set it up so that it will be easy to follow, but it must also be complete enough to give a clear idea of what suggestions involve. Using what you know about proposals, develop a one-page RFP for the company. Then apply what you have learned about design to make it attractive and easy to understand. Be prepared to share your form with the class and to turn it in to your teacher.

- Imagine that you are a sales representative for a firm that submits bids on specific jobs to prospective customers. The jobs might be for plumbing, wiring, or painting—or for the construction or remodeling of an entire house. Your firm might be a group of architects bidding for the design contract on a new city building, or perhaps a group of physicians who want to contract for providing health care to employees of a large corporation. Choose a situation that interests you, and develop a sales proposal that describes the service(s) you would provide, the manner and time frame in which they would be delivered, the qualifications of your firm and those who would be responsible for the project, and the cost. Be prepared to share your finished proposal with the class and to turn it in to your teacher.

- Schedule an interview with a person who works regularly in the area of proposal writing or review. This might be a development officer for a local college or school district, an independent consultant who writes proposals on assignment for nonprofit organizations, or a program officer of a foundation who reviews proposals that are submitted for funding. Develop a set of questions, based on what you have learned in this lesson, and use the interview to refine your knowledge and understanding of proposal writing. Be prepared to share what you learn with the class and to turn in a one- to two-page summary of your interview to your teacher. With your teacher's permission, you may wish to invite the person you interview to visit your class and share his or her insights directly with the other students.

LESSON 13

A Proposal to America

A Literature Lesson

Looking Ahead

What This Lesson Is About

In this lesson, you will read a poem, "Let America Be America Again," by Langston Hughes. This poem contains a proposal for ending inequalities in American life and making the American dream come true.

- ✔ Proposals are not confined to the workplace. They come in many forms, including works of literature.
- ✔ Literary proposals can be highly persuasive even though they may not include all the components of a workplace proposal.
- ✔ Literary proposals can reach a much larger audience than workplace proposals.

The American dream includes the opportunity to find success in the workplace, regardless of a person's gender or race.

component—part of a system

Great Depression—the disastrous world economic downturn that followed the stock market crash of 1929

implement—to carry out, to put in operation

utopia—a visionary place of political and social perfection

Identifying a Problem

Wherever people live in communities, problems are bound to arise. A community without problems would be a utopia—an ideal place with perfect social and political conditions. Think for a few moments about problems in your community—your city, town, or school. Perhaps these problems involve the unfair treatment of certain members of your community. Perhaps powerful members of your community receive special treatment. Choose the one problem that you would most like to see fixed, and write an entry in your journal describing this problem.

Be prepared to read your journal entry in class. Keep it for use later in this lesson.

Getting Started

"Let America Be America Again" by Langston Hughes

During the Great Depression of the 1930s, wide inequalities existed in American life. Many people were out of work, had little to eat, and lost hope that the American dream of success, happiness, and equality for all citizens could ever come true. American Indians had been savagely torn from their homelands; black Americans were not considered as equals by powerful whites but were merely "problems"; and many immigrants, despite their best efforts, could not improve their social and economic position.

At this desperate time, when many writers and politicians were offering serious but conventional proposals for remedying the country's ills, the black poet Langston Hughes offered his fellow citizens a proposal in verse: "Let America Be America Again." In persuasive language, he showed how powerful the dream of freedom could be, even in the face of poverty and despair. More than two decades later, Hughes's words in this and other poems helped inspire the civil-rights movement.

As you read this poem, look for specific measures that Hughes suggests for implementing his proposal.

> We hold these truths to be self-evident, that all men are created equal, that they are endowed by their Creator with certain unalienable Rights, that among these are Life, Liberty and the pursuit of Happiness. That to secure these rights, Governments are instituted among Men, deriving their just powers from the consent of the governed.
>
> —The Declaration of Independence (July 4, 1776)

Meet Langston Hughes

Langston Hughes (1902–1967) was a very productive writer, publishing 10 volumes of poetry and some 60 short stories, as well as many dramas, operas, literary anthologies, and humorous books.

Born in Joplin, Missouri, Hughes attended Central High School in Cleveland, Ohio, then traveled extensively while still a young man. Working as a busboy at a hotel in Washington, D.C., he met the American poet and critic Vachel Lindsay, who encouraged him to make a career as a writer.

Hughes, along with Claude McKay, Countee Cullen, and Zora Neale Hurston, became one of the most important figures in the Harlem Renaissance, the cultural flowering that took place in Manhattan's mostly black Harlem section in the 1920s. Among his books are *The Ways of White Folks*, *Not without Laughter*, *Collected Poems*, and two autobiographies, *The Big Sea* and *I Wonder As I Wander*.

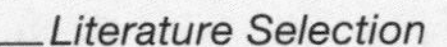

Literature Selection

Let America Be America Again

Let America be America again.
Let it be the dream it used to be.
Let it be the pioneer on the plain
Seeking a home where he himself is free.

(America never was America to me.)

Let America be the dream the dreamers dreamed—
Let it be that great strong land of love
Where never kings connive nor tyrants scheme
That any man be crushed by one above.

(It never was America to me.)

O, let my land be a land where Liberty
Is crowned with no false patriotic wreath,
But opportunity is real, and life is free,
Equality is in the air we breathe.

(There's never been equality for me,
Nor freedom in this "homeland of the free.")

Say, who are you that mumbles in the dark?
And who are you that draws your veil across the stars?

I am the poor white, fooled and pushed apart,
I am the Negro bearing slavery's scars.
I am the red man driven from the land,
I am the immigrant clutching the hope I seek—

pioneer—one of the first persons to settle a land or to investigate a subject

connive—to work together in secret, to conspire

tyrant—a harsh and oppressive ruler

Liberty—freedom personified

equality—the state of being the same or alike

And finding only the same old stupid plan
Of dog eat dog, of mighty crush the weak.

I am the young man, full of strength and hope,
Tangled in that ancient endless chain
Of profit, power, gain, of grab the land!
Of grab the gold! Of grab the ways of satisfying need!
Of work the men! Of take the pay!
Of owning everything for one's own greed!

I am the farmer, bondsman to the soil.
I am the worker sold to the machine.
I am the Negro, servant to you all.
I am the people, humble, hungry, mean—
Hungry yet today despite the dream.
Beaten yet today—O, Pioneers!
I am the man who never got ahead,
The poorest worker bartered through the years.

barter—to exchange goods rather than money

Yet I'm the one who dreamt our basic dream
In that Old World while still a serf of kings,
Who dreamt a dream so strong, so brave, so true,
That even yet its mighty daring sings
In every brick and stone, in every furrow turned
That's made America the land it has become.
O, I'm the man who sailed those early seas
In search of what I meant to be my home—
For I'm the one who left dark Ireland's shore,
And Poland's plain, and England's grassy lea,
And torn from Black Africa's strand I came
To build a "homeland of the free."

serf—a person working under slave-like conditions

furrow—a narrow groove in the ground, as made by a plow

lea—open ground, meadow

strand—shore

The free?

Who said the free? Not me?
Surely not me? The millions on relief today?
The millions shot down when we strike?
The millions who have nothing for our pay?
For all the dreams we've dreamed
And all the songs we've sung
And all the hopes we've held
And all the flags we've hung,
The millions who have nothing for our pay—
Except the dream that's almost dead today.

relief—welfare payments

O, let America be America again—
The land that never has been yet—
And yet must be—the land where *every* man is free.
The land that's mine—the poor man's, Indian's,
    Negro's, ME—

Who made America,
Whose sweat and blood, whose faith and pain,
Whose hand at the foundry, whose plow in the rain,
Must bring back our mighty dream again.

Sure, call me any ugly name you choose—
The steel of freedom does not stain.
From those who live like leeches on the people's lives,
We must take back our land again,
America!

O, yes,
I say it plain,
America never was America to me,
And yet I swear this oath—
America will be!

Out of the rack and ruin of our gangster death,
The rape and rot of graft, and stealth, and lies,
We, the people, must redeem
The land, the mines, the plants, the rivers.
The mountains and the endless plain—
All, all the stretch of these great green states—
And make America again!

Art by Brenda Grannan

Trying It Out

Responding to "Let America Be America Again"

Now that you have read the poem, answer the following questions. Support your answers by citing specific lines of the poem or the information in **Meet Langston Hughes**. Record your responses on a separate sheet of paper.

1 What emotion—sadness, anger, hope, joy, or some other—did you feel most strongly when you read this poem? Why did you feel that way?

2 What problem or problems does this poem seek to solve?

3 What audience is the poet addressing?

4 What purpose does Hughes's proposal serve?

5 What specific references in the poem help make its argument persuasive?

6 What changes, in the poet's opinion, would let America be America again?

Where's the Action?

A careful reading of "Let America Be America Again" shows that, while Langston Hughes vividly describes the problem of inequality in America, his poetic proposal presents no specific ways to bring about the desired changes.

Since Hughes wrote his poem, there has been a long struggle to implement his proposal. A few years after Hughes wrote it, America entered World War II. Shortly after the war, President Harry S. Truman issued an executive order admitting black Americans to the U.S. armed forces on an equal basis with whites. Other steps followed, and soon the civil-rights movement was born.

On a separate sheet of paper, list a few changes that have occurred since 1938 to help equalize the status of blacks, American Indians, women, members of religious minorities, immigrants, and whites. Then complete Hughes's proposal by writing a paragraph recommending steps to implement his ideas. If you wish, express your thoughts in verse.

Be prepared to read and discuss your paragraph in class.

Thoughts from a Member of the Harlem Renaissance

At certain times I have no race, I am me. When I set my hat at a certain angle and saunter down Seventh Avenue, Harlem City, feeling as snooty as the lions in front of the Forty-Second Street Library, for instance. . . . The cosmic Zora emerges. I belong to no race nor time. I am the eternal feminine with its string of beads.

—Zora Neale Hurston, "How It Feels to Be Colored Me," first published in 1928 and reprinted in *I Love Myself When I Am Laughing . . . And Then Again When I Am Looking Mean and Impressive* (Old Westbury, NY: Feminist Press, 1979)

"As one of the dumb, voiceless ones I speak. One of the millions of immigrants beating, beating out their hearts at your gates for a breath of understanding."

—Anzia Yezierska, "America and I," *Children of Loneliness*

Summing Up

Solving the Problem

At the beginning of this lesson, you wrote a journal entry describing a serious problem in your community. Review that entry, and then, in your journal, outline a proposal for solving the problem. As you write, be sure to consider all the elements of proposal writing that you have learned in this module.

Be prepared to read and discuss your journal entry in class.

How to Eat a Poem

by Eve Merriam

Don't be polite.

Bite in.

Pick it up with your fingers and lick the
juice that may run down your chin.

It is ready and ripe now, whenever
you are.

You do not need a knife or fork or
spoon or plate or napkin or tablecloth.

For there is no core

or stem

or rind

or pit

or seed

or skin

to throw away.

Art by Brenda Grannan

Keeping Track

On a separate sheet of paper, answer the following questions. Use what you have learned in this lesson to help you.

1. In what forms may problem-solving proposals be written?
2. How may literary proposals differ from workplace proposals?
3. What is one way that audiences for literary proposals may differ from audiences for workplace proposals?

> ***"We have more provincialism and bigotry and superstition and prejudice per square mile than almost any other nation."***
>
> —Bill Mauldin,
> American political cartoonist

Going Further

- Several decades before Langston Hughes wrote "Let America Be America Again," the white American poet Walt Whitman wrote "I Hear America Singing." Find a copy of Whitman's book *Leaves of Grass*, and read this poem. Then write a paragraph describing at least one way in which the poems of Hughes and Whitman differ and at least one way in which they are similar. Be prepared to share your findings with the class.

- Learn more about the writers of the Harlem Renaissance. One way to do this is by visiting Internet sites devoted to the subject, such as http://www.geocities.com/Athens/Forum/4722/bit.html and http://netnoir.com/spotlight/bhm/literature.html. You can find other sites by using a search engine such as Yahoo! You can also find good sources in your library, including encyclopedias and literary anthologies such as *Voices from the Harlem Renaissance*, edited by Nathan Irvin Higgins. Write a brief essay comparing Langston Hughes and his work with other poets and poetry of the Harlem Renaissance. Be prepared to share your essay with the class.

- Many organizations exist to support causes that they feel will make America a better place to live. Such groups as Habitat for Humanity and the Nature Conservancy propose programs or actions connected with improving the environment or people's living conditions. With your teacher's permission, get in touch with officials from such a group and invite them to send a speaker to tell your class about proposals the organization has supported and how the proposals have been implemented.

The Entrepreneurial Spirit

The 1990 U.S. census report showed that African-Americans' drive for entrepreneurship outpaced the nation's by 20 percentage points, with the number of black-owned firms growing 46 percent between 1987 and 1992. An urban phenomenon, these firms generated $1.7 billion a year in New York in 1992. The second-largest number of black-owned businesses was in Washington, D.C., followed by Los Angeles, Chicago, and Atlanta.

—Adapted from Robert C. Solomon, *The New World of Business: Ethics and Free Enterprise in the Global 1990s* (Lanham, MD: Rowman & Littlefield, 1994)

LESSON 14

Writing Executive Summaries

A Strategies Lesson with Video

Looking Ahead

What This Lesson Is About

In this lesson, you will write an executive summary.

- ✔ An executive summary usually precedes a written proposal or other workplace document. It gives the reader a quick overview of what's in the document.
- ✔ The summary states the main subject of the proposal or the problem at hand. It lists the objectives or probable results of the proposed project and outlines the writer's recommendations or plan for accomplishing the project. It also may state the document's conclusions.
- ✔ Rules of thumb for summary writers include being succinct and clear, omitting most of the proposal's details, using the present tense, paraphrasing rather than quoting word for word, and not adding one's own opinions.

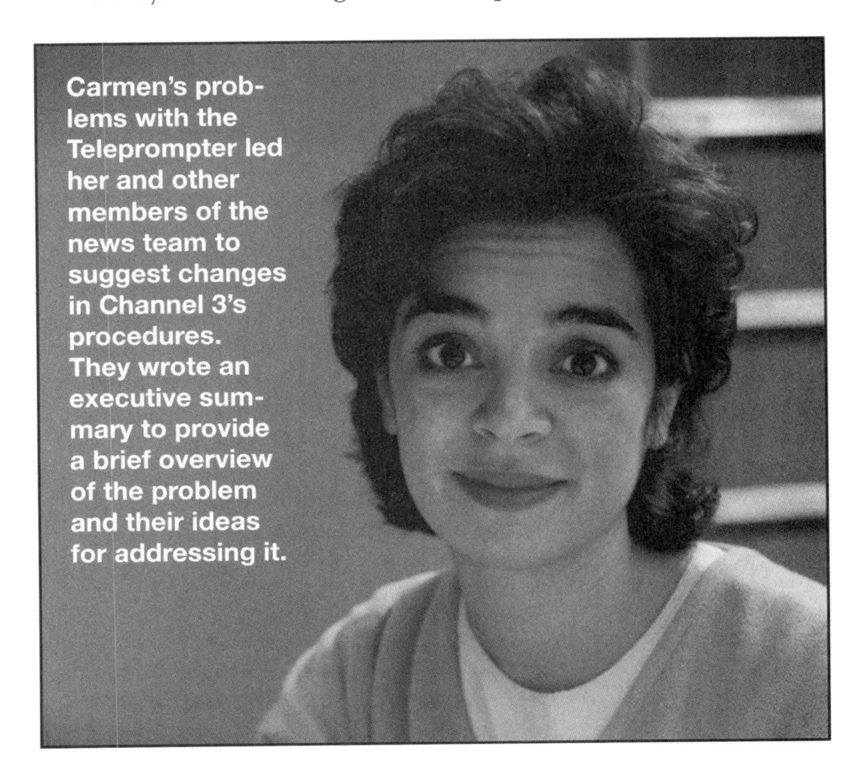

Carmen's problems with the Teleprompter led her and other members of the news team to suggest changes in Channel 3's procedures. They wrote an executive summary to provide a brief overview of the problem and their ideas for addressing it.

clarity—the quality of being clear and easily understood

paraphrase—to restate a text to give the same meaning in different words

succinct—expressed in few words

telegraphic—written in a concise, clipped style resembling a telegram (for example, "Stranded in Topeka. Send money.")

A Person of Few Words

Writing succinctly—using as few words as possible to say what you want to say—is an art that goes beyond basic writing techniques. Perhaps the most highly developed type of succinct writing is haiku. This Japanese poetic form makes a striking statement, usually in three lines of five, seven, and five syllables respectively. Here is an example of haiku:

> A black burly dog
> Bounding over the bluebells:
> Brendan's on the loose.

A lower, but still artful, form of succinct writing is the newspaper headline, for example, "Iowa Couple Welcomes Septuplets" and "Shocker: Colts Defeat Packers." Advertising slogans ("Just Do It") and political sound bites ("Just Say No") are other examples of succinctness.

Try your hand at succinct writing by summarizing, on a separate sheet of paper, the main point made by the following two paragraphs. Although your summary need not be as poetic as haiku verses or as telegraphic as a headline, keep it to one sentence, use as few words as possible, and strive for clarity.

> If you take pride in your writing or designing abilities, you may shudder at the thought of changing a document on which you have worked very hard. Taking pride in your work is good—most successful professional writers do. But don't let your pride keep you from looking objectively at your work or from accepting constructive feedback from people who read it.
>
> Always remember that the most important thing in workplace writing is not your own feelings but the creation of a document that will be of use to someone else. To achieve greater accuracy and appeal, you may need to revise any document you produce.

Be prepared to share your summary with the class and to compare your efforts with those of your classmates. Are the summaries both succinct and clear?

Defining Haiku

Haiku are simple. Often beginners try to put too much into it. A good rule is to have at least two concrete images, no more than three. Some schools of haiku (think of fish) are happy with a couple images which paint a lovely scene wherein your mind can wander and wonder.

—Jane Reichhold, "Another Attempt to Define Haiku," (written for and first posted on the Shiki International Haiku Salon, April 16, 1996) (http://www.faximum.com/aha.d/haidefjr.htm)

Meeting the Challenge of Brevity

The shorter a writing task is, the more challenging it can become, because each word must count. Writing good abstracts and summaries is difficult for three reasons:

1. Writing an accurate, effective abstract or summary requires good reading skills—high comprehension and an understanding of relationships among ideas
2. You have to avoid the temptation to include too much information.
3. An abstract or summary usually requires a great deal of revision to represent the original document accurately.

—Adapted from Rebecca E. Burnett, *Technical Communication*, 3d ed. (Belmont, CA: Wadsworth, 1994)

Getting Started

Writing a Summary: Where, What, and Why

An executive summary usually precedes a workplace proposal or other document. It often stands alone on its own page between the contents page (if there is one) and the first page of the main text of the document. In most cases, the writer produces the summary after writing the entire proposal. An executive summary accompanying a proposal generally has four parts.

- The first part identifies the main subject or problem dealt with in the proposal, preferably in a single sentence.
- The second part briefly reports the objectives or probable results of the project proposed.
- The third part summarizes the writer's recommendations or plan of work to accomplish the project.
- The fourth and final part restates the conclusions of the proposal.

Summaries run from one or two short paragraphs to a couple of pages. The length of the summary depends on the length of the document: the shorter the proposal, the shorter the summary.

The writer provides the summary to give readers a quick overview of the document's subject matter. In one sense, the summary is

The Proposal in Miniature

An executive summary should be short, approximately 10 percent the length of the entire document. Regardless of the length of a proposal, however, an executive summary should not exceed five pages.

An executive summary is the proposal in miniature. It identifies and explains the problem, purpose, proposed plan or procedures, staffing and personnel, costs, evaluation criteria, and the proposed solution. Executive summaries may contain headings and graphics.

The executive summary will be one of the first sections looked for and read by everyone. If it does what it is supposed to do—persuade the reader to read the entire proposal—your proposal will have made it past the first hurdle.

—Joel P. Bowman and Bernadine P. Branchaw, *How to Write Proposals That Produce* (Phoenix: Oryx, 1992)

the most important part of a document, because it helps readers decide whether to read the entire piece of work. Often the summary is the only part of a document that people read. When writing is meant to persuade readers to do something, a well-crafted summary can lead them to read every part of a document closely.

Summaries are especially useful now that many reports are computerized. On a computer, users can instantly preview documents by retrieving and reading their summaries. Most academic and technical journals run summaries (called abstracts) of all their articles.

Using what you have just read, answer the following questions:

1 Where is the executive summary placed in a proposal or other document?

2 What are the four parts of a summary?

3 How does the writer determine the length of a summary?

4 How do computers make summaries even more useful?

Be prepared to discuss your answers in class.

Writing a Summary: How

The two main points to remember when you are writing an executive summary of a proposal or other document are: be succinct, and be clear. Use as few words as possible, and avoid words that may trip up your readers. As with any kind of writing, always keep your readers in mind and choose your words on the basis of their knowledge.

Here are some other rules of thumb:

- Write your summary in the present tense.
- Paraphrase your proposal's contents—do not quote word for word. It is not necessary to follow the proposal's exact order.
- Omit most of your proposal's details, examples, facts, definitions, and explanations. No matter how important you may feel they are, they don't belong in a brief summary.

- Do not include any facts or personal opinions that do not appear in the document. The summary should contain no new information or views.

You can follow these four steps in writing an executive summary for a proposal:

1. In the first sentence, identify the problem that the proposal addresses.
2. In the next sentence(s), outline the objectives or results expected if the proposal is followed.
3. In the next sentence(s), list the writer's recommendations or plan of work to accomplish the objectives.
4. In the last sentence, state the proposal's conclusions.

Using what you have just read, answer the following questions:

1 What are good strategies for writing succinctly and clearly?

2 Why do summaries omit a proposal's details?

3 What are the four steps in writing a summary?

Be prepared to discuss your answers in class.

> ***"Brevity is the soul of wit"***
>
> —William Shakespeare, *Hamlet*
>
> ***"Genius is the ability to reduce the complicated to the simple."***
>
> —C. W. Ceram, quoted by Peter Potter, *All about Success*

For Example

Here is an executive summary that was written to accompany the internal proposal for educational programming at an animal hospital, the full text of which appears in Lesson 11 (pages 105–109). First, quickly read that proposal; then, read the summary.

Executive Summary

[Sentence 1] In response to a recent increase in reproductive surgeries and diversification of the client population, two Raintree Animal Hospital technicians propose to expand the hospital's educational programming and

community outreach. *[2]* The main goals of their plan are to enhance the hospital's image and bolster its client list, to lessen postoperative complications and preventable injuries, and to improve relations with local animal shelters and the city's animal-control program.

[3] The technicians' plan proposes to establish a bureau to provide speakers on veterinary topics at community meetings, conduct hands-on community workshops on pet care and nutrition, develop additional instructional materials for distribution by the hospital and at workshops, and hold periodic vaccination and well-pet clinics throughout the region. *[4]* The plan calls for two experienced hospital employees to manage the program and for volunteers, including present hospital employees, to staff it. *[5]* It thus foresees minimal costs. *[6]* The program can begin as soon as it is approved and a method of evaluation is suggested.

[7] If approved, the program not only can benefit the health and well-being of small animals in the region but also can raise hospital staff morale as employees work together to develop their creativity, presentation skills, and public-relations expertise.

Using what you have just read, answer the following questions:

1 Which sentence or sentences make up the first part of this executive summary? How about the second part? The third part? The fourth part?

2 Does the summary adequately cover the main points in the proposal? Explain your answer with examples.

3 Is the summary succinct and clear? Explain your answer with examples.

Be prepared to discuss your answers with the class.

Trying It Out

The Beginning and the End

If you completed the activities in Lesson 12, you created an internal proposal. Now you will have a chance to write an executive summary to insert in that proposal. Following the steps outlined in **Writing a Summary: How**, use the **Executive Summary** form to write your summary. Keep it succinct—about a third of a page. Then reread what you have written, and do a self-critique.

Carmen's efforts to solve the training problems at Channel 3 will help her fulfill her new responsibilities as a camera operator.

Summing Up

The Whole Shebang

Exchange summaries with another student. Give each other feedback on the summaries by answering the questions at the bottom of the **Executive Summary** form.

If necessary, revise your summary on the basis of the feedback you receive. Then, using a computer program, type the summary as a separate page and insert it in the correct position in your proposal. Verify the position by checking the **Proposal Planning Flowchart** in Lesson 12 (page 115). Save the completed proposal. Print out a copy, and save it in your portfolio.

Be prepared to discuss your executive summary in class.

Epilogue

Search 35459, Play to 36814

Viewing the Videodisc—Epilogue

You are about to watch a video segment that completes the story of the proposal for Channel 3. As you watch, think about how you would solve the new problem that the station faces.

Executive Summary

Use this form to write the executive summary for your proposal to the TV station. Once you have drafted it, critiqued your work, and revised it, ask another student to give you feedback. This person can use the feedback section at the bottom of this form to comment on your work.

Proposal writer's name ______________________________

Part	Executive Summary
1. **Subject** *What is the proposal about?*	
2. **Objectives/Probable Results** *What do you hope to accomplish?*	
3. **Plan or Recommendations** *How will you accomplish your plan or recommendations?*	
4. **Conclusion** *What is your request?*	

Feedback Form

	Yes	No
1. **Are any parts missing?** *If yes, what parts?*	☐	☐
2. **Is the summary succinct?** *If not, how would you edit it?*	☐	☐
3. **Is the summary clear?** *If not, how would you clarify it?*	☐	☐
4. **Is the present tense used?**	☐	☐
5. **Are the points paraphrased rather than quoted directly?**	☐	☐
6. **Are details omitted?**	☐	☐
7. **Are personal opinions omitted?**	☐	☐

Name of reviewer ______________________________

Keeping Track

On a separate sheet of paper, answer the following questions. Use what you have learned in this lesson to help you.

1 What is the main purpose of providing an executive summary in a written proposal or other document?

2 What are the four parts of an executive summary?

3 In writing an executive summary, what are some rules of thumb to follow?

Why Is Workplace Writing Important?

A survey of 265 professional employees at 20 research and development organizations revealed that workplace writing is important because it

- provides answers to specific questions (69%)
- keeps others informed about major activities (60%)
- helps in planing and coordinating the activities of the individual and the organization (52%)
- objectifies a situation so that its essential elements and interrelationships can be analyzed (49%)
- instructs others (47%)
- enables individuals to make contact with others who rank higher inside the organization or outside it
- establishes accountability (38%)

—J. Paradis, D. Dobrin, and R. Miller, *Writing at Exxon ITD: Notes on the Writing Environment of an R&D Organization* (New York: Guilford, 1985)

Going Further

- Creating short poems or song lyrics is a good way to learn to write succinctly, because poets and songwriters must make every word count if they want their work to be effective. Perhaps you have a favorite short poem or song lyric that does this. If not, look through an anthology of verse for a poem that you feel is both succinct and meaningful. Or read the poem "How to Eat a Poem" by Eve Merriam that appears in Lesson 13 (page 131). Using the poem or song lyric you choose as inspiration, create one of your own that is both succinct and meaningful. Be prepared to share your work with the class.

- Abstracts are summaries that often precede articles in academic journals. Two respected medical journals, the *Journal of the American Medical Association* (*JAMA*) and the *New England Journal of Medicine* (*NEJM*), give on-line instructions to would-be contributors on how to write abstracts. You can find the *JAMA* instructions at http://www.ama-assn.org/public/journals/jama/jabstrac.htm (look under the headings "Instructions for Preparing Structured Abstracts," "Reports of Original Data"). The *NEJM* instructions are at http://www.nejm.org/GenRes/text/InfoAuth.htm#Abstracts. Go to these sites, and read both sets of instructions. Then write a brief review describing the two sets and comparing them for succinctness and clarity. Tell which one most resembles the guidelines for summary writing that you learned in this lesson. Be prepared to share your findings with the class.

- In their book *Clear and Simple as the Truth*, Francis-Noël Thomas and Mark Turner applaud what they call "classic prose." This writing style, which aims to mirror truth through clarity and simplicity, has been used by such honored authors as Thucydides (*The Peloponnesian War*), Plato (*Apology*), Samuel Johnson (the *Rambler* papers), Edith Wharton (*A Backward Look*), and Mark Twain (*Life on the Mississippi*). It has also been used by writers of good technical guides (for example, Alan Simpson's *Mastering WordPerfect 5.1 for DOS*, and the Audubon Society's field guide series). Find a copy of Thomas and Turner's book in a library, and read the section on *The Audubon Society Field Guide to North American Birds, Eastern Region* (pages 115–117). Write a one-page report that explains what "classic prose" is and why good technical works such as the Audubon books provide excellent examples of it. Be prepared to summarize your report in class.

"There is a great difference in boats, of course. For a long time I was on a boat that was so slow we used to forget what year it was we left port in. But of course this was at rare intervals. Ferry-boats used to lose valuable trips because their passengers grew old and died, waiting for us to get by. This was at still rarer intervals. I had the documents for these occurrences, but through carelessness they have been mislaid."

—Mark Twain, *Life on the Mississippi*
(Boston: James R. Osgood, 1883)

Proposing a Change

An Application Lesson

Looking Ahead

What This Lesson Is About

In this lesson, you will use what you have learned to develop a proposal that you can later present to an employer in an occupational area that interests you.

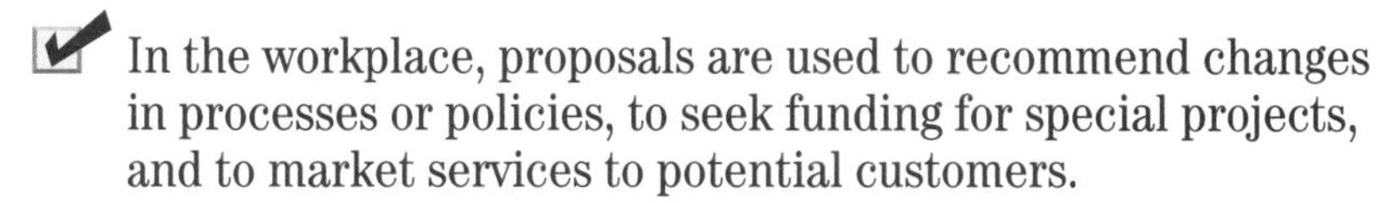

- In the workplace, proposals are used to recommend changes in processes or policies, to seek funding for special projects, and to market services to potential customers.
- Workplace writing uses persuasive techniques, both in content and design, to encourage people to read the document and to convince them to support the proposed actions.
- Two keys to writing effective proposals are knowing the needs and interests of your reader and adapting the content, structure, and design of your proposal to those needs and interests.

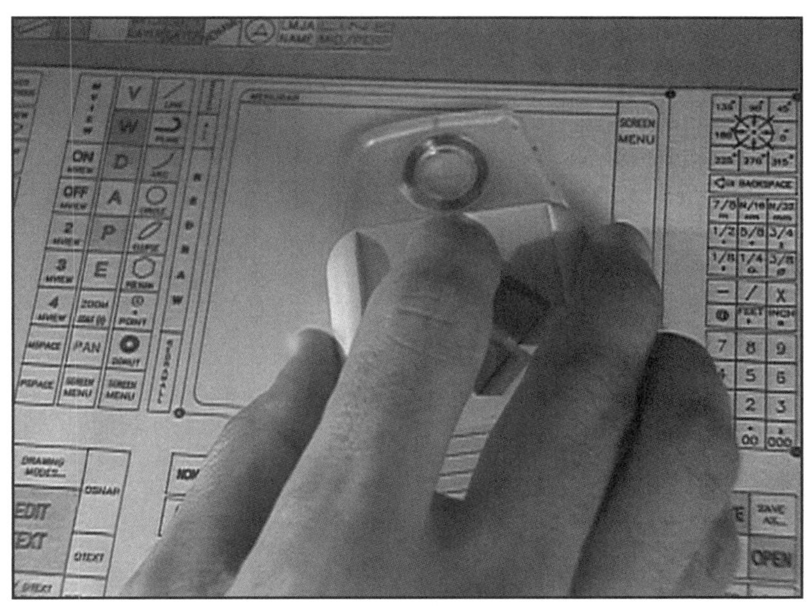

No matter where you work or what you do, your skills in technical communication will help you solve many problems that you may encounter on the job.

Key Ideas

e-mail—electronic mail; written messages entered and delivered through a computer network

survey—a detailed study in which information is gathered by questioning a number of people

The Magic Five

In this module, you have learned a great deal about the content, structure, editorial style, and design of such technical documents as proposals, instructions, and process descriptions. In fact, you may have learned more details than you can remember at one time. Studies have shown that five is the magic number: People have trouble dealing with more than five items of information or five concepts at one time.

Imagine that you are asked to summarize all the key points you have learned about technical communication for a group of new employees. None of these people knows very much about the subject. You don't want to burden them with details, but you want to get across the most important points. Assume that they can master five concepts at your first session. Review what you have learned, and develop a list of five rules for technical communication to share with them. Be sure that the points are relevant to proposals and other forms of writing that are often part of proposals, such as instructions and process descriptions.

When you have completed your list of five key rules, be prepared to share them with the class and to defend them as the most important things to know about technical communication.

Getting Started

Writing at Work

If you have completed the earlier activities in this module, you analyzed a proposal written by two employees in an animal hospital and you wrote a proposal to the operations manager of a TV station. Of course, you may have no intention of becoming a vet tech or working in a TV station. Maybe you're going into engineering, farming, or construction. Perhaps you plan to work in a hospital. Or you may be planning to go into business for yourself. In some fields, you'll never need to write a proposal . . . or will you?

You may be surprised to learn that, even in fields where people don't think much about good writing, most employees are routinely required to write memos, e-mail messages, and occasional letters. What's more, a great many of these employees—many of them only a few years out of school—also must write proposals of some type. Suppose, for example, you conducted an e-mail survey about proposal writing. The following are some typical responses that you might receive. They illustrate three situations in which proposal-writing skills are needed in the workplace.

> ***"I could go out and operate any machine that I wanted to, but if I couldn't write about it properly, I wouldn't be able to communicate that to anyone else. . . . So I would say that my writing skills are probably the most important skills that I have."***
>
> —Roy White,
> technical writer, Boeing

Date: Fri. 22 Nov 1998 19:00:04 -0500 (EST)
From: "Ryan Neal" >rneal@homebuild.com
To: back@AIT.net
Subject: Proposals

I'm a licensed electrician, and never expected to write anything more than my signature on a paycheck when I went to work for HomeBuilders, Inc. Little did I know!

From the start, I had to write simple proposals to tell prospective clients what wiring I intended to do, how much it would cost, and how long the job would take to complete. I got to be pretty good at that, and it's a good thing I did. Now that I'm operations manager for the company, I have to do proposals for whole house renovations. That means pulling together the information from all the craftsmen—plumbers, electricians, painters, carpenters, all those guys who think they can't write—and creating a proposal that will get us the job.

Of course, we all know that if we don't do a good job, we won't get the next contract. But the fact is, we'll never get a chance to prove how good we are if that first proposal isn't a winner. Fortunately, proposal-writing skills—like any skills—improve with use. Each one I write is a little better than the one before.

Date: Wed. 20 Nov 1998 9:23:12 -0700 (EST)
From: "Jessica Cline" >kcline@rehab.edu
To: back@AIT.net
Subject: Proposals

I knew that nonprofit organizations like the rehabilitation facility I work for depend on grants from outside organizations. But I didn't know that, as a physical-therapy aide, I'd be writing proposals for those grants. Actually, I

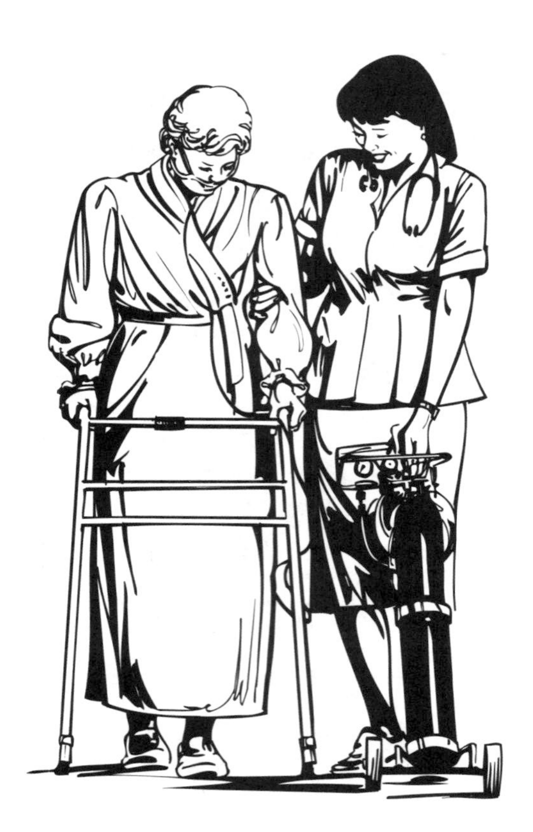

don't usually write the entire proposal. But when the development director gets to the description of the process we use to help stroke patients regain mobility, she always asks me to write the narrative. I also keep case notes that we use to document the importance of regular therapy in the rehabilitation process of all our patients.

I really enjoy working on these proposals. I've learned so much that I could probably write the whole document now, if I had to. And, of course, the motivation is there: these grants pay my salary!

Date: Mon. 25 Nov 1998 13:16:09 -0800 (EST)
From: "Geraldo Diaz" >hdiaz@PAT.gov
To: back@AIT.net
Subject: Proposals

What does a bus driver know about proposal writing? Usually, not very much, but when I wanted to submit my idea for revamping the Transit Authority's method of scheduling drivers for holiday runs, I learned about it in a hurry. I was told that nobody would hear my suggestion unless I put it into a proposal.

Well, the short version of a long story is that I figured out how to put my thoughts together in a simple proposal, management bought my idea—in fact, they loved it—and now I'm a division manager. And guess what! Part of my job is to help prepare the annual proposals to the state for the public-transit subsidy grants.

I've always been more into the mechanics of things than into writing about them, but I've found I can do both. Half the battle of writing about a process or giving instructions to somebody is understanding the mechanism.

The situations that Ryan, Jessica, and Geraldo describe could occur in almost any workplace. What's more, they represent the three most common types of workplace proposals—the sales proposal and bid, the external proposal to a funding source, and the internal proposal to recommend policy or procedural changes within an organization.

Using what you have read, answer the following questions:

1 What type of proposals does Ryan write?

2 Is Jessica involved in writing external or internal proposals?

3 In what way is Geraldo's first proposal (about the change in scheduling) different from those he now is working on for submission to the state?

Be prepared to share your answers with the class.

Trying It Out

> *"Plans get you into things, but you got to work your way out."*
>
> —Will Rogers, American actor and humorist

Choosing Your Audience and Your Product or Service

In this lesson, you will develop a proposal to submit to a supervisor, a potential customer, or a funding source, such as a foundation. The plan you develop will address an identified problem or need in an occupational field that interests you. Most of you are probably considering careers in one of these areas: agriculture/natural resources, mechanics and transportation, business and computer technologies, health and human services, engineering technologies, construction and design, or communication technologies.

Choose one of these fields or another one that interests you, and identify a situation in which you are called upon to write a proposal. Some possible situations appear in the table on the following page. Use one of them, or—with your teacher's approval—devise a topic of your own.

When you have selected an occupational area and a situation that requires a proposal, follow these steps to develop the proposal:

1 **Create the scenario.** Describe your employer and the need or problem you have identified. Decide who will receive the proposal: give the name and position of the person within the company for an internal proposal or the name of the customer or funding source for an external proposal. Summarize the situation in a one-page scenario. You may be asked to share this scenario with the class or with your teacher before you proceed with your research.

2 **Research the problem.** Review Lessons 2 and 3 on planning and information gathering. Spend time researching your field and your specific problem by talking with people who work in the field. Look up information in books and magazines in the library, or browse the Internet.

3 **Plan your proposal.** Using a copy of the **Proposal Planning Flowchart** (Lesson 12, page 115), determine whether you have all the information you need for each section. If you don't, go back to your information sources and fill in the empty spots.

Send an Inquiry before Making a Proposal

An increasing number of funders prefer brief letters of inquiry concerning the suitability of a match between your proposal and their interests before you submit a full proposal. A letter of inquiry should touch on all the elements that would eventually be part of a proposal; it should be no more than two pages long and should indicate what the next step will be (for example, that you will follow up with a phone call within two weeks). The objective of a letter of inquiry is to get the funder to invite you to submit a proposal.

—*The Foundation Center's User-Friendly Guide to Funding Research and Resources*, Internet Edition

In this occupational area . . .	. . . you may choose to write a proposal that
AGRICULTURE/ NATURAL RESOURCES	• urges that the farm where you work begin planting buffer strips along bordering riverbanks to reduce erosion • bids on the contract to supply fresh produce, dairy products, and poultry for the county's nursing and personal-care facility for the elderly
MECHANICS/TRANSPORTATION	• requests foundation funding to make city buses accessible to people with disabilities • suggests that the auto-repair shop where you work offer training courses in basic car maintenance to its customers
BUSINESS AND COMPUTER TECHNOLOGIES	• bids on the maintenance contract for computers and copiers in a large corporation • suggests that sales reps have training in repair and maintenance to improve their understanding of how the machines work
HEALTH AND HUMAN SERVICES	• requests foundation funding to provide medical services to the homeless • recommends developing a collaboration with a local college to offer student internships (which would expand the service capacity of the agency)
ENGINEERING TECHNOLOGIES	• recommends that your company create a summer program to introduce disadvantaged children to engineering careers • recommends developing periodic updates for all engineers on changes in code regulations
CONSTRUCTION/DESIGN	• bids on the plumbing (or electrical) work rehabilitating 12 rowhouses near the downtown business district • recommends that work schedules be developed one to two months in advance to reduce absenteeism and overtime.
COMMUNICATION TECHNOLOGIES	• recommends that a cable-TV company expand its program options to attract more subscribers and to compete with satellite-to-home services • seeks funds for a public television special for children about HIV and AIDS

4 **Write your proposal narrative.** Be sure you have answered all the key questions. In describing the approach you would take to solving the identified problem or filling the need, you can follow the guidelines for writing a process description presented in Lesson 11. Prepare your narrative on the computer, and take advantage of the design strategies given in Lessons 8 and 9 to make the document attractive, readable, and easy to understand.

5 **Prepare sample materials.** Does your proposal call for the development of instructions, training, or procedures related to the operation of a specific piece of equipment? If so, develop a sample instruction sheet and/or mechanism description to include in the attachments. If you plan to include a detailed project budget, staff résumés, or other information in the attachments, create these items.

6 **Create a title page, and write a one- or two-paragraph summary** of your proposal. The information contained in Lesson 14 can help you with this part of your proposal.

7 **Collect all the parts of your proposal**, and arrange them in the proper order. Then make two copies—one for your portfolio and one to exchange with another student for feedback.

Power Up with Planning

1. Identify the problem or goal. Ask who, what, when, where, why, and how?
2. Identify the solution. Collect ideas through brainstorming.
3. Divide the solution into tasks, and gather the necessary information.
4. Create a schedule for completing the tasks. Assign the time needed to complete each task and meet the deadline.

Summing Up

Getting and Giving Feedback

Using copies of the two-page **Proposal Review** form (Lesson 12, pages 121–122), evaluate the proposal of the student with whom you exchanged documents while he or she evaluates yours. In addition to responding to the "Yes" and "No" questions, offer suggestions for improving the proposal.

Be constructive in your suggestions, and be prepared to back up any criticisms you make with information from other lessons. When you receive the review of your proposal, consider the comments and suggestions; then revise your proposal, and incorporate the suggestions that you consider appropriate. Save your proposal. Print out a final copy of it to turn in to your teacher, and keep a copy in your portfolio.

Be prepared to discuss your reactions to the evaluation with the class.

> ***"The best way to improve your writing is to have others review and comment on it."***
>
> —Douglas Wieringa, Christopher Moore, and Valerie Barnes, *Procedure Writing: Principles and Practices* (Columbus, OH: Battelle Press, 1993)

Going Further

- Arrange to visit a work site in an occupational field that interests you. When you schedule your visit, explain that you particularly want to meet with employees who are responsible for technical communication. Prepare several questions about the role that writing plays in this field. Ask whether proposal writing is a regular or an occasional task—and whether the proposals are usually internal or external. Summarize what you learn in a one- or two-page paper. Be prepared to share your paper with the class and to turn it in to your teacher.

- "Editorials in newspapers and magazines are often mini-proposals. Read several editorial pages in your local newspaper and in national newsmagazines and/or trade journals from an occupational field that interests you. Choose one or two editorials that suggest a change in a governmental policy or process. Analyze the editorials to see whether they answer all of the key questions that proposals should answer. Summarize your findings in a one- or two-page paper. Turn in the editorials and your paper to your teacher.

- Proposals are not limited to e-mail, letters, memos, and lengthier reports. Another kind of proposal is a résumé with a cover letter. This type of proposal addresses a prospective employer's problem (the need for additional help) by providing a solution (your skills and experience). You can create an effective résumé and cover letter by following the same steps that help you write other proposals—these steps are listed in **Trying It Out**. Using the Internet and other resources, look for a job in the occupational area that interests you. Then develop a one-page summary that explains how you would use the seven-step process for developing a proposal to apply for the job. Where would you find information about your occupational area? Where would you find current job listings? And where would you find information on companies looking for help? List the resources you find in your report. Be prepared to share your job listing and your proposal-writing strategy with the class.

Web Work

Look for information on career exploration and current job openings on the World Wide Web. Here are some Web sites to check.

Career Exploration Links—Occupational: http://www.uhs.berkeley.edu/careerlibrary/links/occup.cfm

***Occupational Outlook Handbook*, 1994–95** (click on "Occupational Coverage"): http://www.claitors.com/ooh/ooh00001.htm

ETA Career Exploration: http://www.doleta.gov/individ/careerex.htm

4Work: http://www.4work.com/

JobSmart: http://jobsmart.org/

JobHunt: http://www.job-hunt.org/

Glossary

active voice—sentence structure in which the subject performs the action

audience—persons who will hear or read what you say or write; persons who will be affected by your decisions

brainstorming—the unrestrained offering of ideas by members of a group seeking to solve a problem

bullets—small typographic symbols (usually dots, diamonds, or squares) used to set off items in a list

caution—indication of potential conditions that could damage the equipment or injure the operator

chronological—in the order of time, from first occurrence to last

chunking—grouping related ideas together

clarity—the quality of being clear and easily understood

component—part of a system

data matrix—a graphic device or table for recording information in a systematic way

draft—the preliminary form of a document that will be revised

e-mail—electronic mail; written messages entered and delivered through a computer network

ethical responsibility—an obligation determined by personal or generally accepted standards of conduct

evaluation—assessment; measurement of accomplishment

feasibility report—a document that defines a problem, offers criteria for solving it, suggests possible solutions, and then recommends the best solution

feedback—information obtained from reader response to a document

flowchart—a diagram showing the progress of a process in sequential order

font—a specific typeface, distinguished by the style of the letters, numbers, and other characters; traditional printers use the word "font" to refer to a specific size of the typeface (for example, 12-point Helvetica), but today the terms "font" and "typeface" are often used interchangeably

Great Depression—the disastrous world economic downturn that followed the stock market crash of 1929

highlighters—variations in a typeface, used to draw attention to specific words or phrases

imperative mood—sentence structure in which the reader or listener is commanded to do something

implement—to carry out, to put in operation

irony—the use of words that say the opposite of what the speaker or writer means

justification—the process of spacing out lines of type so that the ends of the lines are even

labeling—using headings or subheadings to identify sections of a document or topics within a section

legal requirement—required by law, with appropriate penalties or punishment for failing to comply

memo (or memorandum)—an informal written message, usually sent within an organization

objectives—aims, goals

parallel construction—the use of the same grammatical structure in a series of related statements

paraphrase—to restate a text to give the same meaning in different words

persuasive—having the power to convince other people to do or believe something; in a proposal, persuasiveness takes the form of a logical argument based on facts and sound reasoning

pocket reminder—a brief list of key steps from a set of instructions; these steps are used to stimulate the memory of someone who knows how a process works but may need to be reminded

point—a unit of measurement for type (one point is approximately 1/72 of an inch)

proposal—a persuasive document suggesting a solution to a problem or need

rationale—reason or justification for performing a task

relevant—related to, pertinent

reliable—dependable, trustworthy, authoritative

Request for Proposals (RFP)—a formal announcement or notice that funds are available to organizations that can provide specific services or products; a request lists the requirements that proposals must meet, the deadline for submitting proposals, and the place where they must be sent

retailer—a person or business that sells goods or articles directly to consumers

revision—the corrected and improved form of a draft document

sans serif type—typeface (font) without the decorative "tails" (serifs)

sarcasm—irony that is deliberately harsh

satire—a literary work, usually delivered in a tone of irony, that makes fun of or scorns human foolishness or error

serif type—typeface (font) with tiny fine lines (or "tails"), usually on the tops or bottoms of letters

spontaneous—without thought or planning

succinct—expressed in few words

survey—a detailed study in which information is gathered by questioning a number of people

synthesize—combine various elements into a whole

technical communication—an oral, visual, and/or written process that informs an audience about the details of a topic

telegraphic—written in a concise, clipped style resembling a telegram (for example, "Stranded in Topeka. Send money.")

timely—up-to-date, recent

tombstoning—an unintentional alignment of headings in two adjoining columns

tone—the style or manner in which a person speaks or writes

utopia—a visionary place of political and social perfection

warning—indication of potential hazards that may cause serious injury or death

white space—areas in a document (margins, space between columns, or portions of the page) that contain no graphics or type

widow—an incomplete line of type that falls at the top or bottom of a column

Additional Resources

Books

Burnett, Rebecca E., *Technical Communication* (Belmont, CA: Wadsworth Publishing Company, 1997).

Ewald, Helen Rothschild, and Rebecca E. Burnett, *Business Communication* (Upper Saddle River, NJ: Prentice-Hall, 1997).

Ferrari, Cosmo F., *Writing on the Job* (Englewood Cliffs, NJ: Prentice-Hall, 1995).

Freed, Richard C., Shervin Freed, and Joe Romano, *Writing Winning Business Proposals* (New York: McGraw-Hill, 1995).

Harcourt, Jules, A. C. "Buddy" Krizan, and Patricia Merrier, *Business Communication* (Cincinnati: South-Western Educational Publishing, 1996).

Hyden, Janet S., Ann K. Jordan, Mary Helen Steinauer, and Marjorie J. Jones, *Communication for Success: An Applied Approach* (Cincinnati: South-Western Educational Publishing, 1994).

Mehlich, Sue, and Darlene Smith-Worthington, *Technical Writing for Success: A School-to-Work Approach* (Cincinnati: South-Western Educational Publishing, 1997).

Miculka, Jean H., *Let's Talk Business: A Speech Communication Text* (Cincinnati: South-Western Educational Publishing, 1993).

Literature

Commoner, Barry, "Three Mile Island Catastrophe," *The Politics of Energy* (New York: Knopf, 1979).

In this short essay, the author uses the reporter's "5 Ws and an H" to describe how a near meltdown occurred at a nuclear plant in Pennsylvania.

Keillor, Garrison, "Attitude," *Happy to Be Here* (New York: Atheneum, 1982).

America's "tallest radio comedian" gives instructions on how to act like a winner in baseball even when you're losing.

Laviera, Tato, "AmeRícan," *The American Reader: Words That Moved a Nation,* ed. Diane Ravitch (New York: Harper Perennial, 1991).

In this poem, Puerto Rican-born Tato Laviera shares his vision of a new generation that can embrace the possibilities of reconciliation and pluralism in America.

Swift, Jonathan, *A Modest Proposal* (1729).

Considered to be a masterpiece of irony, this widely anthologized pamphlet recommends that the terrible suffering in Ireland be relieved by having the poor raise their children to be killed and sold as food.

Videos

We strongly suggest you preview all videos.

Apollo 13, directed by Ron Howard (Universal City, CA: MCA Universal, 1995). Starring Tom Hanks, Bill Paxton, and Kevin Bacon. (2:20)

Based on actual events, the heroic rescue of three astronauts depends on the ground crew's ability to develop and communicate instructions for making needed repairs.

Broadcast News, directed by James L. Brooks (Los Angeles: Fox Video, 1987). Starring William Hurt, Holly Hunter, and Albert Brooks. (2:12)

This behind-the-scenes movie provides insight into how news anchors, producers, and reporters interact as they create television news broadcasts.

Online Resources

American Communication Association Grant and Fellowship page—http://www.uark.edu/depts/comminfo/www/grants.html

Federally Funded Research Projects—http://medoc.gdb.org/best/fed-fund.html

The Foundation Center—http://fdncenter.org

Online services can be used to enhance instruction, increase resources, and discuss issues with other educators throughout the world. Many online services offer a trial period, ranging from a few free hours to a month's membership. Members may choose from a variety of plans, including several designed for a multiuser, educational environment. When considering which online service to use, consider local Internet providers. Access fees for these new companies may be competitive with those of larger providers, and local firms may also provide quicker access.

The five most popular national providers have designed part of their service for educational use. These providers are:

America Online
800/827-6364

CompuServe
800/848-8199

Delphi Internet Services Corporation
800/695-4005

GEnie Services
800/638-9636

PRODIGY Service
800/PRODIGY (800/776-3449)

Acknowledgments

Literature and Audio Acknowledgments, Module 13

"How to Poison the Earth" by Linnea Saukko, from *The Bedford Reader,* 6th ed., edited by X. J. Kennedy, Dorothy M. Kennedy, and Jane E. Aaron (Boston: Bedford Books, 1997). Print and audio copyright ©1997 by St. Martin's Press, Inc. Reprinted with permission of St. Martin's Press, Inc.

"Let America Be American Again," from *Collected Poems* by Langston Hughes. Copyright ©1994 by the Estate of Langston Hughes. Reprinted by permission of Alfred A. Knopf, Inc. Audio recorded by permission of Harold Ober Associates, Inc. Copyright ©1994 by the Estate of Langston Hughes. Photo copyright ©1930 by Consuelo Kanaga. Courtesy of the Estate of Wallace B. Putnam, by Alfred A. Knopf Publicity.

"Hand-Held Can Opener," adapted from *Technical Writing for Success: A School-to-Work Approach* by Sue Melich and Darlene Smith-Worthington. Copyright ©1997 by South-Western Educational Publishing, a division of International Thomson Publishing, Inc. All rights reserved. Reproduced with permission.

"How to eat a poem," from *A Sky Full of Poems* by Eve Merriam. Copyright ©1964, 1970, 1973 by Eve Merriam. Copyright renewed. Reprinted with permission of Marian Reiner.

Photographs, Illustrations, Graphics Acknowledgments, Module 13

All photos used by permission of the Agency for Instructional Technology and/or the author, except where noted.

All illustrations and graphics used by permission of the Agency for Instructional Technology, except where noted.